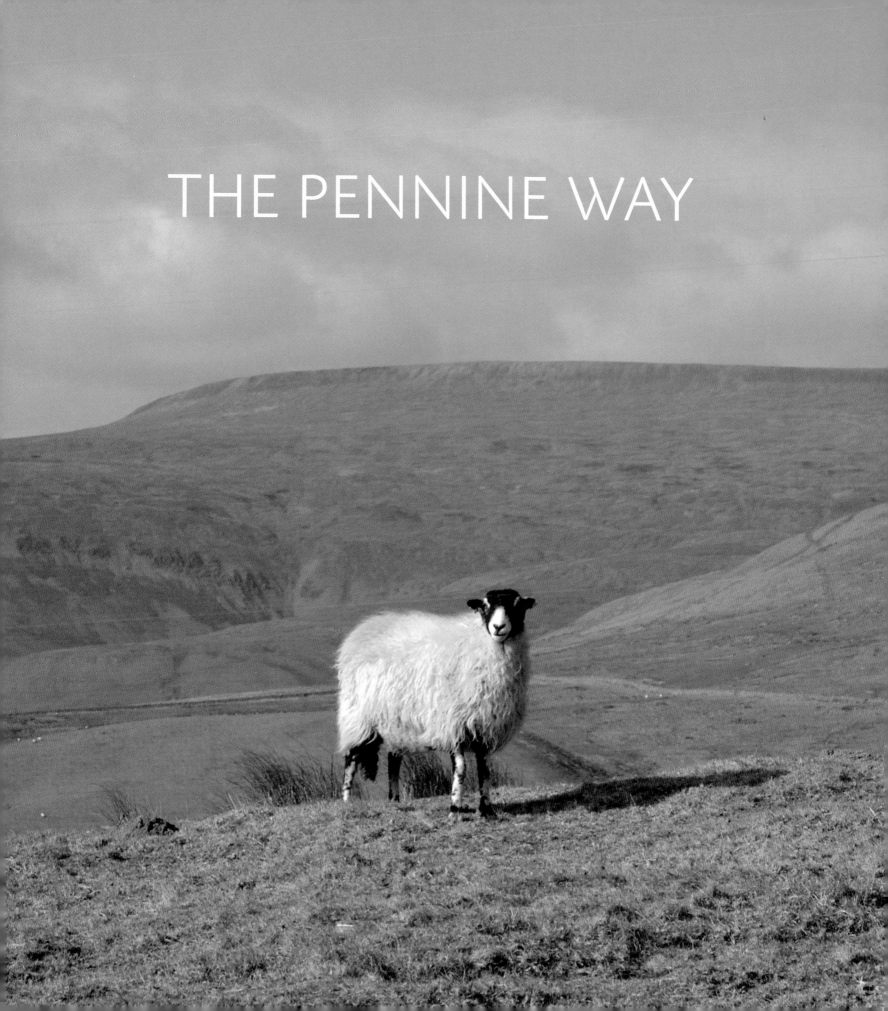

THE PENNINE WAY

THE PENNINE WAY

Roly Smith

Photographs by John Morrison

F

FRANCES LINCOLN LIMITED

PUBLISHERS

This book is dedicated to the abiding memory of Tom Stephenson, who made it his Way.

The Pennine Way
Frances Lincoln Limited
4 Torriano Mews
Torriano Avenue
London NW5 2RZ
www.franceslincoln.com

ISBN: 978-0-7112-3024-8

Printed and bound in China

9 8 7 6 5 4 3 2 1

HALF TITLE A sheep poses in front of Cross Fell, the highest point on the Pennine Way.

TITLE PAGE A cairn pierces the gloom in Ribblesdale.

CONTENTS

INTRODUCTION:
A LONG GREEN TRAIL

'A Short Walk With Tom'
From *Peak Park News*, journal of the Peak
District National Park, Autumn 1976:

*'Aye,' said Tom, a warm smile creasing his weatherbeaten face.
'It's a grand valley isn't it?'*

*We were looking up Grindsbrook Clough to the rock-rimmed
Edale Moor. This was where it all began. The Pennine Way snakes
northwards for 250 miles from here to beyond the Scottish Border,
keeping to the upper vertebrae of England's backbone all the
way.*

*But when Tom Stephenson proposed, in a throwaway centre-
spread filler for the* Daily Herald *forty-one years ago, 'a faint line
. . . which the feet of grateful pilgrims would engrave on the face of
the land,' he could have had no idea of what would follow.*

*Doesn't the four-lane 'motorway' which the feet of those
grateful pilgrims have worn in the eleven years since the final
adoption of the Pennine Way offend him now?*

*'Not at all,' he said. 'It's no more ugly than the peat groughs
or scree slopes on Kinder, and it's just as natural as a sheep track.
The whole idea was that the Pennine Way should not be a "made"
path; "no concrete or asphalt track", as I said in the original
article.*

*'No,' he said looking down at the 'motorway,' 'this doesn't
offend me – Constable would have loved it, it adds a bit of colour
to the valley.' He was less than complimentary, however, about the
black plastic matting recently laid north of the Snake Summit.*

* * *

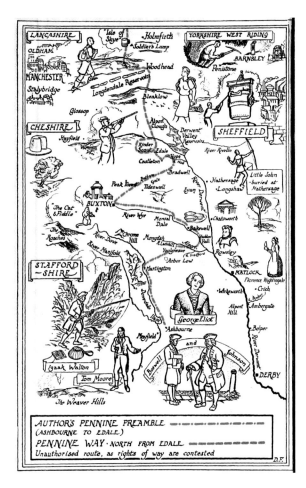

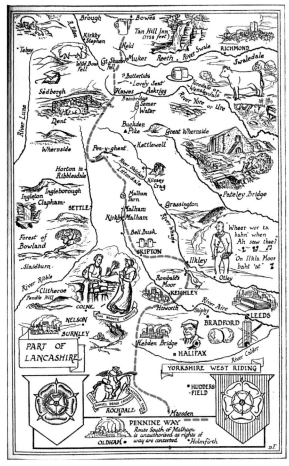

LEFT Pennine Way creator Tom Stephenson poses by one of his hated trespass signs.

RIGHT Illustrative maps of the proposed Pennine Way by Donald Foster, from the endpapers of John Wood's 1938 classic, *Mountain Trail*.

BELOW A peat grough on Bleaklow.

RIGHT The author with Tom Stephenson on the Pennine Way in Grindsbrook, 1976.

Tom, a sprightly, impish eighty-three, was back at Edale as a speaker during the Footpath Preservation conference at Losehill Hall. He took time off to see his beloved Way after an absence of about twelve months.

'The way I feel, this route has given so much pleasure to so many thousands of people who perhaps otherwise would not have ventured onto the hills,' said Tom. 'This is what I wanted in the first place, and when I see young people enjoying themselves on the Way, it makes it seem worthwhile.'

But there had been a mounting wave of criticism in mountaineering circles against the designation of all forms of long-distance footpaths. The proposed Cambrian Way and a long-distance route in the Cairngorms had attracted a storm of protest. Were there not too many 'ways' now?

'Mountaineers were always opposed to the Pennine Way,' he recalled. 'The Times complained that ramblers were being mollycoddled when the Pennine Way was first proposed. But having a designated "way" has meant more people enjoying the freedom of the hills, and I can't see anything wrong in that.' But he added: 'Perhaps the time has come when we have got enough.'

* * *

Talking to Tom about the inception of the Pennine Way, and the setting up of the National Parks Commission, you realize how important a part fate plays in these things. He was the right man in the right place at the right time. It is doubtful whether any of this important legislation would have passed onto the Statutes had not all these conditions have been in place at the time.

Tom's face lights up and his tongue darts out mischievously as he recounts the tales of a judiciously worded press release written with carte blanche Ministerial consent, or the publicity-seeking walks with leading MPs and Ministers along sections of the Pennine Way; all arranged when he was Press Officer to the Ministry of Town and Country Planning just after the war. 'Aye, we had some fun,' he grins.

* * *

He frankly admits that one of the major reasons for the route was to clear up the longstanding and knotty problems of access over Kinder and Bleaklow. When the route was first proposed, there were 180 miles on existing rights of way, leaving about 70 miles of new rights of way to be negotiated. Half of these were in the Kinder-Bleaklow section. Tom has some horrifying tales to tell of the old access battles fought between ramblers and gamekeepers on the moors of the

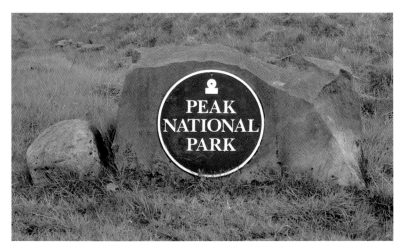

Peak National Park boundary marker.

Dark Peak, and still keeps a dossier of gamekeeper assaults during that period.

It was an incredible seventy years ago that Tom had his introduction to the hills. He climbed Pendle Hill from his home in Whalley, Lancashire, one crisp February morning, 'equipped' only with his wooden clogs, and stood for the first time on a summit. The memory of that crystal-clear morning is still as fresh to Tom as if it were yesterday.

'It was breathtaking,' he recalled. 'I saw range after range of snow-capped hills – Ingleborough, Penyghent, all of which I didn't know then, but which were to become old friends.

'Oh gosh, I just hadn't realized that this whole new world was on my doorstep. I made up my mind that day that this was for me.'

* * *

The nine-bob-a-week apprentice textile printer walked the Pennines from Dovedale to the Roman Wall during the next seven years, and got to know them intimately, although he admits he still hasn't walked the whole length of his Pennine Way in one continuous trip.

Seventy years on, the attraction of the hills is still as strong. He was looking forward to a walking holiday in the Lakes when we met, keenly anticipating a reunion with his favourite hill, Glaramara – 'not too high, but nice and knobbly.'

A recent television documentary renamed the Pennine Way 'Stephenson's Way', and it is a fitting tribute to his imaginative conception to say that this was no exaggeration.

* * *

The preceding is an account of my first meeting with Tom Stephenson, the man whose brilliant idea the Pennine Way was; the man who fought for thirty years to make it, and our National Parks, happen; the man who became both my hero and my mentor as I pursued my own career, paralleling but never remotely equalling his, in outdoor journalism and the conservation of the countryside.

What I remember most about Tom, who died at the age of ninety-four in 1987, were his unshakeable principles. One in a long line of northern autodidacts, and a declared pacifist, he had to give up a hard-won scholarship in geology to the Royal College of Science (now Imperial College) in London when he became a conscientious objector during the First World War. After two courts martial, he was imprisoned for his beliefs and spent two years in the claustrophobic cells of Wormwood Scrubs and Northallerton.

This was the same man who after the war became a campaigning outdoor journalist, editing such journals as *Hiker and Camper* and *Out of Doors*, before joining the staff of the socialist newspaper, the *Daily Herald*, in 1933 where he became a regular columnist and outdoor correspondent.

This was the man who went on in 1943 to become Press Officer to Minister Lewis Silkin at the Ministry of Town and Country Planning, just as John Dower's seminal report on National Parks and Access to the Countryside, including Long Distance Paths, was being written. Tom found the Ministry 'a cheerless place permeated with a fear of publicity'. But in John Dower he discovered 'a kindred spirit' and was delighted to be given the heaven-sent opportunity of publicizing his report, which of course eventually led to the National Parks and Access to the Countryside Act of 1949.

This was the man who, after he left the Civil Service in 1948, became the honorary secretary of the Ramblers' Association for twenty-one years, helping it to make it the 140,000-member, professional and media-savvy organization it is today.

This was the man who led MPs and Cabinet Ministers on a publicity-attracting walk in May 1948 from Teesdale to Birkdale and High Cup Nick, and then from Cross Fell up to Hadrian's Wall, along his proposed Pennine Way. They included the recent Chancellor of the Exchequer Hugh Dalton, Barbara and Ted Castle, Arthur Blenkinsop, Julian Snow, George Chetwynd, Geoffrey de Freitas and Fred Willey, who seventeen years later was to perform the opening ceremony for the Pennine Way. Of course, many of that immediate post-war Labour Government were ramblers already – some of them even trespassers – and didn't take much persuasion.

Barbara, later Baroness, Castle commented later: 'Tom knew how to use politicians. He got a number of us led by Hugh Dalton to come and help him blaze the trail – the physical trail and the trail of publicity up over Cross Fell – and I was struck by his unobtrusive professionalism.

'Just to see Tom sit down and put on his walking boots gave me confidence. We politicians brought the panache, but Tom organized the route, guided us over the slippery slopes and got us there.'

And this was the man who in December 1986 was eventually to receive his just reward when he was awarded an honorary degree of Doctor of Law by the University of Lancaster. The Public Orator described him as someone 'to whom all those who walk for recreation in this country owe an inestimable debt'.

* * *

The story of how the *Daily Herald* received a letter from two American girls asking for advice about a walking holiday in England is well known. They wondered if we had anything similar to their Appalachian Trail, which runs for 2,000 miles from Maine to Georgia, or the John Muir Trail, running for 2,500 miles from the Canadian border through Washington, Oregon and California.

Tom's seminal article in response, headed 'WANTED – A Long Green Trail' and published on 22 June 1935, proposed 'a Pennine Way from the Peak to the Cheviots'. He explained: 'This need be no Euclidean line, but a meandering way deviating as needs be to include the best of that long range of moor and fell; no concrete or asphalt track, but just a faint line on the Ordnance Maps which the feet of grateful pilgrims would, with the passing years, engrave on the face of the land.'

It was, and still is, a great idea, but Tom's hidden agenda was to use his proposal for a Pennine Way as a lever to open up the long-forbidden moorlands of the Peak and South Pennines. In those days, around 50 square miles of Kinder Scout and Bleaklow – the highest ground in the Peak – were uncrossed by any right of way and barred to walkers.

These were the scenes of the great access battles of the 1930s, and although Tom never approved of the well-publicized Mass Trespass on Kinder Scout in 1932 (he and leader Benny Rothman never saw eye-to-eye), like most northern ramblers he was an inveterate trespasser himself. But he found himself in complete agreement with the sentiments expressed in Ewan MacColl's famous song, 'The Manchester Rambler' – which Tom always said was the best thing to come from the mass trespass:

> No man has the right to own mountains
> Any more than the deep ocean bed

TOP The plaque in Bowden Bridge Quarry, Hayfield, which celebrates the 1932 Mass Trespass.

ABOVE Tom Stephenson's seminal article from the *Daily Herald*, 22 June 1935.

The trouble was, since the Enclosure Acts of the eighteenth and nineteenth centuries, landowners *did* own our mountains and moorlands. These vast areas of open country which had previously been common land were stolen from the people and converted to exclusive grouse moors for the enjoyment of the privileged few. The other fierce opponents of the proposed Way were the water authorities, who feared pollution to the water supplies in their catchment areas from ramblers. It is not recorded what they felt about the thousands of defecating sheep and grouse.

These forbidden lands were jealously guarded by those gamekeepers, often armed with sticks and guns,who were so graphically described by MacColl in his song. They were not averse to using strong-arm tactics to remove trespassing ramblers, and those in the Peak were reckoned to be among the worst.

It took Tom and his fellow members of the Pennine Way Association and National Parks Commission three long decades of dogged persistence and patient negotiation to overcome those objections. But the Pennine Way was finally opened by Fred Willey, then Minister of Land and Natural Resources, at a ceremony attended by Tom and 2,000 other ramblers held at Malham Moor on 24 April 1965 – ironically thirty-three years to the day after the Kinder Mass Trespass.

The first guidebook to the official Pennine Way was published in 1960 by Manchester schoolteacher Kenneth Oldham, who had led the first school party to complete the route in 1951. But one of the finest accounts of the route had been published thirteen years before that with John Wood's *Mountain Trail*, beautifully decorated by Donald Foster's elegant pen-and-ink drawings.

The book was dedicated to Tom and other officers of the Pennine Way Association, and interestingly, Wood starts the route in Dovedale and finishes it by following the Harthope Burn down into Wooler. This southern extension to the start of the Pennine Way was to become a constant cause of argument in the years to come, and in the north the approved route eventually turned northwest from The Cheviot to cross the Border and descend into Kirk Yetholm.

Tom wrote the first official HMSO guide to the route himself in 1969, a book handsomely illustrated by Harry Titcombe's drawings, which were later to grace the original covers of the Ordnance Survey 1:25,000 Outdoor Leisure maps. Easily the most popular guide, Alfred Wainwright's idiosyncratic *Pennine Way Companion*, had been published the previous year.

Wainwright, dogged by bad weather as he completed the route in sections, scarcely concealed his dislike of the Pennine Way. In his conclusion he said he hoped that others would enjoy the Way because it would do them good. But he added: 'You won't come across me anywhere along the Pennine Way. I've had enough of it.' And in describing his own long-distance footpath creation, *A Coast to Coast Walk* (1973), he concluded: 'I finished the Pennine Way with relief, the Coast to Coast Walk with regret. That's the difference.'

Among many misfortunes on the Pennine Way, AW had to be rescued by a National Park warden from sinking without trace in a bog on the summit of Black Hill, and on Cam Fell, a freezing, gale force, east wind 'so shrivelled some of the body organs necessary for a full and enjoyable life that I feared they were perished forever.'

But he did pay a full and glowing tribute to Tom Stephenson in his *Companion*. 'Officially, Whitehall created the Pennine Way. But those who walk it should remember that it was one man who inspired, in his mind and by his patience and effort, the freedom they enjoy.

'Mr Stephenson has served the cause of walkers well throughout a long life, but his name will be most revered for his imaginative conception of a continuous way for travellers on foot across half of England.'

Inevitably, record-breakers were attracted to the route, which, according to the latest official guides by Tony Hopkins, is 256 miles long. The current record for completing the Pennine Way is held by fellrunner Mike Hartley, who ran the route in 2 days, 17 hours, 20 minutes, 15 seconds, in July 1989. Apparently, he ran the whole way without stopping for sleep and halted only twice, for a rather precise 18 minutes each time. He did prove himself to be human, however, because one of his stops was for fish and chips in Alston (which must have slowed him down a bit), and he ran the last 40 miles with a borrowed size 10 shoe on his size eight right foot.

It's now reckoned that the Pennine Way is completed by around 2,000 people every year, and most follow Tom Stephenson's and AW's example by doing it in sections over a number of years. Add to that the huge number of day walkers from the surrounding towns and cities who use parts of the route at some point, and it has resulted in serious problems of erosion, especially on the more popular sections.

Footpath erosion may not have worried Tom thirty years ago but by the mid-1970s, the footpath, National Trust and National Park authorities (it passes through three, the Peak District, Yorkshire Dales and Northumberland) along the route were becoming increasingly concerned about the ever-spreading, braided paths, especially across sensitive and internationally rare blanket bog peat moorland. In some places on Kinder and Bleaklow, for example, the path had become 30 metres wide in places, as walkers stepped aside to find

The photographer, pretending to be lost on Black Hill.

The route up to Kinder has been consolidated with flagstones.

relatively drier ground, and the effects on the precious moorland vegetation and its associated wildlife were becoming unsustainable.

The southern start of the Way through Grindsbrook Meadows, where I walked with Tom thirty years ago, had been worn into a six-lane 'motorway', which the local ranger Gordon Miller delighted in describing as 'three lanes north, three lanes south'. (On another occasion with another ranger, we were horrified to see a smartly dressed couple dressed in about-town clothes walking up this same stretch of the Pennine Way, both carrying a suitcase in each hand. 'How far are you going?' we enquired. 'All the way,' they blithely replied.)

It was clear that something had to be done, and some unfortunate and short-lived experiments such as the looped black plastic matting from the Snake Summit on Bleaklow; the use of bundles of birch palings, and metalled paths 'floated' on sheep fleeces (as used by the Romans 2,000 years before) were employed to try to find a solution. Worried by making the path from the main road too attractive and easy, thus tempting people onto the moor who were not equipped or fit enough to be there, large boulders known as 'granny stoppers' were placed across the path. This unfortunate name managed to be sexist and ageist at the same time, and was soon dropped.

Finally, it was realized that there was no substitute for doing the job properly, and in the case of making a sustainable path across peat moorland, that meant flying in the raw material by expensive, £1,000-an-hour, helicopter. Gritstone slabs, recycled from former textile mills on either side of the Pennines, were ideal for the task, and nowadays they are usually floated on geotextile mats

to prevent them from sinking, like the unfortunate Wainwright, into the morass.

There was an initial outcry from the purists when these measures were introduced – and they did look slightly urban and incongruous at first. But once they have weathered in and the surrounding vegetation has grown back, the results are not displeasing, and very similar to the old packhorse 'causeys' or causeways which have crossed the moors for hundreds of years.

The Pennine Way and other long distance paths (now known as National Trails) now have their own management plans, budgets and dedicated National Trail Officers, charged with their upkeep and maintenance. And they are now promoted by their umbrella authority, Natural England, as 'the best of British walking'.

And what about the Pennine Way in the twenty-first century? Well it can no longer be said to be a challenge in navigation skills, as some of the more popular sections are now paved and the rest of the route is quite unmistakeable. And there is plenty of comfortable bed and breakfast accommodation along the Way to ease your progress. But it still represents the oldest and toughest of Britain's long distance walking routes, and as these beautiful pictures from John Morrison show, there is still no finer way to get to understand the real, gritty character of the north of England.

THE BACKBONE OF ENGLAND:
THE PENNINE PALIMPSEST

The familiar name of the Pennines is a literary forgery executed in the eighteenth century by an English professor teaching in Denmark. Charles Julius Bertram (1723–65) claimed to have discovered a fourteenth-century chronicle, entitled *De Statu Britanniae* and said to be written by a cleric named Richard of Cirencester, which allegedly described Britain as it was in Roman times.

The ingenious Bertram invented many Roman-sounding names, among which was *Alps Penina*, describing the long range of hills which dominates the north of England, presumably to correspond with the Apennines back in the Romans' homeland of Italy. Amazingly, many of Bertram's other mock-Latin inventions can still be found on maps or in guidebooks, such as the Roman camps at Chew Green, just as you reach the Border fence on the Pennine Way, which are still sometimes referred to as *Ad Fines* – literally meaning 'the end of the world.' Not quite the end of the world perhaps, although it may have seemed so to Agricola's legions, but the start of Scotland and the last lap of the Way.

Before the forgery was revealed, two pioneering geologists, William Conybeare and William Phillips, perpetuated the myth by naming the range of hills 'the Penine Chain' in 1822. That name, with the modern addition of an extra central 'n', has been in use ever since, although modern geographers frown upon it, claiming quite correctly that the Pennines are more of a 'broad uplift' than a proper mountain chain.

The earliest written description of the Pennines comes from William Camden, the Elizabethan historian and antiquary, who described in his *Britannia*, first published in 1586, a range of hills in northern England which ran:

> . . . like as Apennine in Italy, through the middest of England, with a continued ridge, rising more and more with continued

tops and cliffs one after another ever as far as Scotland. Here they are called 'Mooreland,' after a while the Peake, Blackstone Edge, the Craven, the Stainmore and at length Cheviot.

Over four centuries later, all these names still have a familiar ring, not least to Pennine Wayfarers. The Staffordshire Moorlands still form the south-western fringe of the 'Peake', now the Peak District National Park, which became Britain's first in 1951. Blackstone Edge, which Daniel Defoe dubbed 'the English Andes' still frowns down on Rochdale and the few remaining chimneys of industrial west Lancashire, and Craven is still the name used for the glorious limestone scenery of North Yorkshire.

Stainmore, the ancient trans-Pennine pass where Eric Bloodaxe met his death in AD 954, is now threaded by the constant roar of traffic on the A66 between the Eden valley and the Vale of York, and the Cheviot still forms the bald, peaty, battle-scarred boundary between the English and the Scots.

In Camden's day, the Pennines were still largely unexplored, and the earliest travellers crossed them with more than a little fear and trepidation. Celia Fiennes, the daughter of a Roundhead colonel from Wiltshire, rode alone and by side-saddle across the Pennines in 1697. She claimed that the country was 'full of steep hills, and nothing but the peakes of hills as thick one by another is seen in most of the County (Derbyshire) which are very steepe which makes travelling tedious, and the miles long'. She also visited Blackstone Edge, which she said was 'noted all over England for a dismal high precipice and steep in the ascent and descent on either end; it's a very moorish ground all about'. She could have been talking about the entire Pennine Way.

Daniel Defoe, in his *Tour Through the Whole Island of Great Britain* published in 1725, famously described the Peak as 'a waste and howling wilderness' and the southern Pennines as 'perhaps the most desolate, wild and abandoned country in all England'. And on Blackstone Edge he was caught in a freak blizzard in the middle of August. He complained: 'It is not easy to express the consternation we were in when we came up near the top of the mountain; the wind blew exceeding hard, and blew the snow directly in our faces, and that so thick that it was impossible to keep our eyes open to see our way.' But we must remember that Defoe was a southerner and not used to Pennine summers . . .

The Pennines have inspired generations of writers and artists since then, from Wainwright to Wordsworth and from Turner to Priestley. The extraordinary flowering of talent which arose from the grim parsonage in the West Yorkshire milltown of Haworth, just off the Way, is unsurpassed in British literature. Anyone who reads the powerful novels of Charlotte, Emily and Anne Brontë cannot fail to see where their inspiration arose.

Perhaps the finest of the novels produced by this trio of precocious sisters was Emily's *Wuthering Heights*, which she published under the pseudonym of Ellis Bell in 1847. In the preface to the 1850 edition, Charlotte describes how to Emily 'her native hills were far more to her than a spectacle; they were what she lived in, and by, as much as the wild birds, their tenants, or as the heather, their produce. She found in the bleak solitude many and dear delights; and not the least and best-loved was – liberty.'

Perhaps it was Glyn Hughes, the Cheshire-born writer who lives close to the West Yorkshire moors, who came closest to capturing the place of the Pennines in northern hearts. In his *Millstone Grit*, published in 1975, he wrote:

> The Pennines thrill with a powerful, special beauty. Out of
> some old neglected industrial town, you may climb a hill and
> be in a world that seems pristine, utterly untouched. In the
> ever-changing light, the shifting peat bogs that are formless
> as putty seem like the soft and shapeless mass of the earth
> before anything was created upon it.

Proud Yorkshireman J.B. Priestley described the long tradition of walking across these northern moors in his *English Journey* (1933):

> However poor you are in Bradford, you need never be walled
> in, bricked up, as around a million folk must be in London.
> These great bare heights, with a purity of sky above and
> behind them, are always there, waiting for you.

The Brontë Parsonage, Haworth.

And Patrick Monkhouse, the stylish deputy northern editor of the *Guardian*, described how the attraction of the moors had always exerted a poweful influence on northern lives. He claimed in his *On Foot in the Peak*, published in 1932:

> The movement which has brought young townsfolk out on
> to the moors has hardly a parallel elsewhere in Britain. For
> an hour on Sunday mornings it looks like Bank Holiday in
> the Manchester stations, except that families do not go to
> Blackpool for Whit-week in shorts. South-countrymen gasp
> to look at it.

Philosopher, Brains Trust regular and access campaigner Professor C.E.M. Joad claimed in *The Untutored Townsman's Invasion of the Countryside* (1946) that in his day, walking had replaced beer as the shortest cut out of Manchester. Alfred Brown, in *Moorland Tramping in West Yorkshire* (1931) estimated that 20,000 ramblers left Manchester every Sunday morning, heading for the moors.

And it is still true that a well-equipped walker clad in anorak, breeches and boots and toting a rucksack would not merit a second glance in Manchester's Deansgate, Leeds's Headrow or Sheffield's Fargate, whereas such a figure would certainly attract attention, and probably not a little derision, in London or Bristol.

Poet Laureate Ted Hughes wrote what could have been a paean to the Pennine Way in his poem 'Where the Millstone of Sky', featured in his *Remains of Elmet* (1979):

> Where the millstone of sky
> Grinds light and shadow so purple-fine

And has ground it so long

Grinding the skin off earth
Earth bleeds her raw true darkness

A land naked now as a wound
That the sun swabs and dabs

Where the miles of agony are numbness
And harebell and heather a euphoria

Painters have also been struck by the dramatic light and bleakness of the Pennines. James Ward's 1812 apocalyptic oil painting of Gordale Scar, ferocious White Park bull in the foreground, is now in London's Tate Gallery. It reflects the then-current fascination with the Gothic horrors of the picturesque. Joseph Mallord William Turner (1775–1851), the English Romantic landscape painter whose style is said to have laid the foundation for Impressionism, made several sketching tours of the Pennines, but unfortunately, no major paintings of the subject.

And the organic, rounded shapes of many of sculptor Henry Moore's works are also said to have been inspired by the wind-blasted gritstone tors of places like those found on his native Yorkshire Moors, and on Kinder Scout and Bleaklow.

Moore (1898–1986) was born in Castleford and in his autobiographical *Henry Moore: My Ideas, Inspiration and Life as an Artist* (1986), he recalls finding a big gritstone tor in Adel Woods just outside Leeds, which influenced him greatly:

It had no feature of recognition, no element of copying of naturalism, just a bleak, powerful form, very impressive.

Nature produces the most amazing varieties of shapes, patterns and rhythms . . .

I am trying to add to people's understanding of life and nature, to help them open their eyes and to be sensitive. Nature is inexhaustible. Not to look at and use nature in one's work is unnatural to me. It's been enough inspiration for two million years – how could it ever be exhausted?

* * *

Except for a few inliers of older rocks, the 'broad uplift' of the Pennines is formed in the main by three distinctive types of rock, each of which creates its own distinctive landforms. All these date from the Carbon-iferous period, an almost unimaginable 300 million years ago, when the land which was to become Britain was considerably closer to the Equator.

Under these semi-tropical conditions, corals, sea lilies and other sea creatures lived and died in huge numbers, gradually floating to the sea floor as they died and building up the great mass of limestone which underlies and forms the bleached white skeleton of the Pennines. This limestone, the country which the poet W.H. Auden memorably claimed was the landscape 'that we the inconstant ones, are constantly homesick for' is exposed today in the White Peak of Derbyshire and the Craven district of North Yorkshire.

Then the mud and sand of the delta of an enormous river system flowing from the north spread and covered the limestone just as the sea floor was slowly sinking. Sometimes this river was fast flowing, leaving extensive sand flats, while at others, when the rate of subsidence was quicker, only fine mud reached the sea. Alternating with the limestones still being created in clearer waters, these sandstones and shales formed the familiar stepped Yoredale series of the Yorkshire Dales – named after the old name for Wensleydale. It also gives us the distinctive *lion couchant* profile of hills like Pen-y-ghent and Ingleborough.

Finally, more rivers flowing from another supercontinent spread more gritty deposits of sand and mud over the area to a depth of over half a mile – creating the distinctive edges of millstone grit, so loved by climbers and previous to that, to makers of millstones and grindstones – hence the name. The summits of the highest hills on the Pennine Way, including Kinder Scout, Bleaklow, Pen-y-ghent, Great Shunner Fell and Cross Fell, are all capped by this impervious layer of millstone grit, creating conditions ideal for the formation of sphagnum moss, the fluffy cotton-wool-ball drifts of cotton grass, and eventually the notorious, ankle-sucking blanket bogs of the high Pennines.

The 'broad uplift' of the Pennines took place relatively recently during Tertiary times (around 30 million years ago) when the rocks were forced upwards by movements deep in the earth's core. This gave us the so-called Derbyshire Dome in the Peak District, a shallow arch formed by the sandwich of successive layers of limestone, shale and gritstone, in which the upper layers in the centre have been gradually eroded away, exposing the limestone of the White Peak. The clints and grykes of the limestone pavements of the Yorkshire Dales were largely the result of the work of Ice Age glaciers, scraping off that final covering of grit and shale.

Volcanic incidents, such the granite and andesite of the Cheviots and the Whin Sill which forms the foundations of Hadrian's Wall, High Force and Cauldron Snout, were merely transitory although spectacularly violent interludes in the long, mainly sedimentary history of the

Clints and grykes in limestone country.

Pennines. But each have contributed their unique landscape features to the Pennine Way, and each add their own distinctive movements to the overall symphony of scenery.

The abrasive effect of Ice Age glaciers broadened the Pennine river valleys and truncated some of them into impressive vertical crags, such as those which can be seen at Malham Cove and High Cup Nick. This happened only yesterday in geological terms, finishing perhaps a mere 10,000 years ago.

* * *

The underlying rocks not only create the scenery, but also the habitats for the wildlife, be it flora or fauna, which make its home there. With the peat-based moorland on the boggy millstone grit plateaux constituting the majority of the route, the Pennine Way has often been described as a wilderness walk. In fact, nothing could be further from the truth.

For a start, the barren and bleak-looking moorlands were, like almost everywhere else in this crowded little island, the result of the hand of man. The thousands of years of human activity started with the earliest Neolithic hunter-gatherers, who were the first to clear and burn large areas of the uplands of their native tree cover to create clearings where they could set up temporary shelters to hunt game. Then came the protected medieval hunting forests, like Langstrothdale Chase in North Yorkshire, and later the lead miners of Swaledale. The modern managers of the moors are the gamekeepers who still regularly burn – or 'swale' – the heather to create an ideal habitat for red grouse and the ubiquitous grazing sheep. Mankind has shaped the Pennines as surely as he has built the mills and industrial cities on either side.

So when you send up a cackling grouse in the heather as you tramp across Kinder or Bleaklow, or perhaps are lucky enough to spot a peregrine falcon as you pass beneath the eponymous Falcon Clints in Upper Teesdale, you should remember that the habitat which supports these wildlife highlights are only there because man's control of the landscape has allowed them to be. The paved Pennine Way is just the latest intrusion.

It is the limestone of the Yorkshire Dales and Upper Teesdale which provide the floral highlights of the Pennine Way. The beautiful and now sensitively managed hay meadows of Swaledale and other dales in the Yorkshire Dales National Park are truly a national treasure, bright with the wildflowers of golden buttercups, globe flowers and scarlet ragged robin, which bloom in drifts around the distinctive field barns where the sweet hay was once stored.

The Upper Teesdale National Nature Reserve has been called 'the valley of the ice flowers', and was only partially saved when the unsightly Cow Green Reservoir was constructed in the 1960s. Here in spring and early summer you will find flowers which have survived from the Ice Age: the startling intense blue of gentians, the delicate pink of the bird's eye primrose (which is also found in the Yorkshire Dales), the sunshine yellow of mountain saxifrage and the creamy-white candles of alpine bistort.

There is a certain spartan beauty to be found in the Pennines, as John Morrison's photographs so eloquently show. But just like the route of the Pennine Way, it is one which has been constantly shaped and moulded by man across a landscape which has been written over time and time again. You could call it the Pennine palimpsest.

The Great Whin Sill outcrops on Hadrian's Wall.

HIGHLIGHTS OF THE ROUTE

The Seven Wonders of the Way
- Kinder Downfall: the 100-foot waterfall which gave its name to Kinder Scout
- Stoodley Pike: a gritstone exclamation mark punctuating the South Pennines
- Malham Cove: once a waterfall higher than Niagara
- High Force: the awesome plunge of the Tees over the Whin Sill
- Caldron Snout: a colossal cascade below Cow Green
- High Cup Nick: the Grand Canyon of Cumbria
- Hadrian's Wall: marking the northern edge of the Roman world

In this chapter we embark on a discursive ramble along the Pennine Way, picking out what for many walkers are highlights of a route which, it must be admitted, passes over bleak and featureless moorland for about half its length.

When I took that short walk with Tom Stephenson thirty-odd years ago, the official route of the Pennine Way left the Nag's Head in Edale

Where it all begins: the Old Nag's Head, Edale.

village and crossed the Grinds Brook by what was at the time a famous log bridge, before winding up through the meadows, crossing Golden Clough, and heading up into the narrowing confines of Grindsbrook Clough.

The scramble up onto the Kinder plateau was a pretty stern baptism of fire for many virgin Wayfarers, and the next stretch across 3 miles of the featureless peat bogs of Kinder Scout, where the only landmarks are the deep groughs ('gruffs' or drainage channels) and hags (banks of peat), were a challenge for even the hardiest of bogtrotters. There are even tales of immaculately equipped and confident virgin Wayfarers setting out from Edale bright and early in the morning, only to return the same evening covered in peat and utterly demoralized – and firmly believing that they had reached Crowden!

The decision to change the authorized route to what was originally called 'the bad weather alternative' – below the landslips of Broadlee Bank Tor to Upper Booth and then up Jacob's Ladder and over the desertscape of Kinder Low (2,076ft/633m) and along the western escarpment to reach the Downfall – was taken partly to ease pressure on the precious blanket peat and partly to provide a more sustainable alternative. It is now paved for much of the way and, as this book was going to press, the National Trust announced plans to erect a 12-mile fence around about five square miles of Kinder's summit as a further anti-erosion measure, to keep sheep – not ramblers – out.

Jacob's Ladder is on an ancient packhorse route between Edale and Hayfield, and it was named after one Jacob Marshall, who lived at the now ruined Edale Head House. He would send his loaded pony up the easier bridlepath while he ascended the steps of his 'ladder'. The direct route was sensitively restored by the National Trust's High

Ascending Jacob's Ladder, Edale.

Peak estate in the 1980s. When broadcaster Brian Redhead opened it he claimed it blended in so well that 'it looked as if it had been constructed in the Iron Age'.

Eventually you reach the Downfall, the major landscape feature – some would say the *only* landscape feature – of note on Kinder. At around 100ft/30m high, it is the highest waterfall in the conspicuously waterfall-less Peak. And it is most famous for flowing backwards on itself, when a strong south-westerly breeze is funnelled up the valley of the Kinder River from Hayfield. In the right conditions, this extraordinary phenomenon can be seen as far away as Stockport, and in these circumstances, as you cross the top of the waterfall, you can enjoy the unique experience of getting wet from above and below at the same time.

Usually however, in these days of global warming, the Kinder River is nearly dry and a mere trickle seeps over the edge. Gone are the days when in most hard winters the Downfall would freeze into a solid curtain of ice, giving ice climbers a rare opportunity to practice their skills in the Peak District, and creating a luminescent, fairytale cave in its lee.

Interestingly, the mountain of Kinder Scout probably takes its name from this waterfall. Literally translated from its Celtic roots, the name *Kyndwr Scut* appears to mean 'water over the edge' – a pretty accurate description of Kinder Downfall in spate. The First Edition Ordnance Survey map of 1864 clearly uses the name Kinder Scout to describe the distinctive nick in the western face of the mountain where the Kinder River flows over the escarpment.

Even the grumpy old Wainwright was grudgingly impressed by Kinder Downfall. He described it as 'a rocky ampitheatre of cliffs and tumbled boulders at the point where the River Kinder reaches the rim of the plateau. The scenery is spectacular.'

Kinder Downfall is also notorious for its voracious sheep, which if you don't watch out, will steal your sandwich as soon as you put it down. The scavenging sheep are well aware that this spot is a kind of Piccadilly Circus for Kinder Scout; a popular meeting and lunchbreak picnic stop for local bogtrotters. You won't see crowds like this again until you reach Malham.

After leaving Kinder by descending the restored, pitched staircase at Ashop Head, the next landmark is the crossing of the A57 Snake Road, well known to listeners to winter weather forecasts and, at 1,600ft/512m, one of the highest points on any major road in the country. Ahead lies Bleaklow, the second highest mountain in the Peak, and one which frequently lives up to its harsh-sounding name.

The route follows the drainage ditch of the Devil's Dyke and through the hidden valley of Hern Clough to reach Bleaklow Head (2,076ft/633m), a peaty summit usually marked only by a stake stuck in a pile of stones. Then you begin the long descent down Torside Clough and along Clough Edge and into Longdendale.

In the valley below the Castles, isolated Alport Castle Farm is the scene of an annual Love Feast. This is no rural rave-up, but a Methodist ceremony involving the consumption of cakes and water in a barn where John Wesley once preached.

Wainwright was again typically uncharitable about Longdendale, calling it 'a mess' and perhaps even worse, 'Manchester-in-the-country'. But at least there are signs of civilization in the welcome shape of Crowden Youth Hostel, after 15 miles of unrelenting boghopping relieved only here and there by paving slabs brought in by helicopters.

Alport Castles, Bleaklow

Alport Castles, in one of the Peak's most remote dales on the southern slopes of Bleaklow, is claimed to be Britain's largest landslip. Its tottering towers and castellated piles would seem to be more at home in the red rock deserts of Utah or Arizona than the green recesses of Alport Dale in Derbyshire.

The landslip was caused by the unstable shales of Birchin Hat slumping away from the daleside to create this crazy pile of gritstone blocks, dominated by the castle-like Tower, which gives the outcrop its name. Now the home of rare birds of prey such as the peregrine falcon, these shape-shifting stones are one of the few places in the Peak where you can actually see natural erosion taking place, as blocks of stone regularly tumble from the rockfaces.

The Huddersfield Narrow Canal at Tunnel End, Marsden.

The next highlight, usually encountered at the start of the second day's travelling, are Laddow Rocks, which are ascended on the long climb out of Crowden Great Brook. Laddow has a special place in Peak District climbing and mountain rescue history and was one of the first places in the country where the sport of rock climbing was undertaken by pioneers like J.W. Puttrell, Siegfried Herford and Ivar Berg.

It was also the place where, in 1928, a member of Manchester's Rucksack Club named Edgar Pryor fell and broke his leg. A makeshift stretcher was constructed using a farm gate and a metal rucksack, and the casualty was carried by his mates the 2 miles down to Crowden. As a direct result of the incident, the Rucksack and Fell and Rock Climbing Clubs formed in 1933 what was called a Joint Stretcher Committee, which was set up to design a suitable stretcher for mountain rescue, which became known as the Thomas stretcher. The committee later developed into the first Mountain Rescue Committee, an organization which generations of climbers and walkers – including many Pennine Wayfarers – have had cause for grateful thanks.

You'd be hard-pressed to call Black Hill, the next major eminence on the route (1,908ft/582m), a highlight. 'It is not the only fell with a summit of peat,' wrote Wainwright, 'but no other shows such a

Last of the Summer Wine Country

The countryside around Holmfirth and Meltham is inevitably associated with the long-running TV comedy *Last of the Summer Wine*, first shown on BBC1 in 1973 and now broadcast in more than twenty-five countries. It's thought to be the longest-running comedy TV programme in Britain and the longest-running TV sitcom in the world.

Mostly filmed in and around Holmfirth, the plot centres around three old men who, despite their years, refuse to grow up. The original trio consisted of Bill Owen as the scruffy Compo, Peter Sallis as the deep-thinking Clegg, and Michael Bates as authoritarian Blamire. Another constant character was the fearsome battleaxe Nora Batty (played by the late Kathy Staff), with her famous wrinkled stockings, the object of Compo's thwarted desire.

Love or loathe the programme, you can't avoid *Last of the Summer Wine* when you are in Holmfirth. Next door to the famous and instantly recognisable venue of Nora Batty's Steps (complete with a pair of Compo's wellies!), you can tuck into home-baked cakes and cream teas at the Wrinkled Stocking Tea Rooms, which is also home to the Last of the Summer Wine Exhibition, just off the Huddersfield Road. Here you can relive the unlikely adventures of the terrible threesome, trace some of the venues which were used, and meet some of the other memorable characters from the long-running comedy.

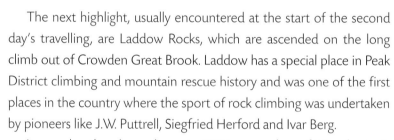

desolate and hopeless quagmire to the sky.' It was here that the inde-fatigable fellwanderer had to be ignominiously dragged out of a peat bog by a passing National Park warden as he researched his *Pennine Way Companion*. Never was a companion more welcome to the solitary old fellwanderer, one suspects.

Nowadays, however, thanks to agencies like the National Park, Moors for the Future and the National Trust, the way to the peaty summit of Black Hill is paved by slabs recycled from millyards – a perfect example of sustainable restoration. The correct name for the summit of Black Hill, by the way, is Soldier's Lump. This was because in the late-eighteenth century, members of the Corps of Royal Engineers originally used the spot for a triangulation point on the first Ordnance Survey. When the mound on the summit (now long eroded away) was exacavated in 1841, the framework timbers for the 36-inch Great Ramsden theodolite used in the original triangulation were found, and are now preserved in the Science Museum in London.

More restored tracks lead you on, crossing the busy A635 Manchester–Huddersfield road at Wessenden Head and past the unnatural, man-made landscapes of the Wessenden Reservoirs to reach another major road crossing over the A62 at Standedge. Here the highlights are largely unseen, as the Standedge Railway and Canal Tunnels, on the Manchester–Huddersfield line and the Huddersfield Narrow Canal between Marsden and Diggle respectively, are far beneath your feet.

On Millstone Edge you are passing over one of the narrowest parts of the Pennines – which hereabouts are a mere 2 miles in width.

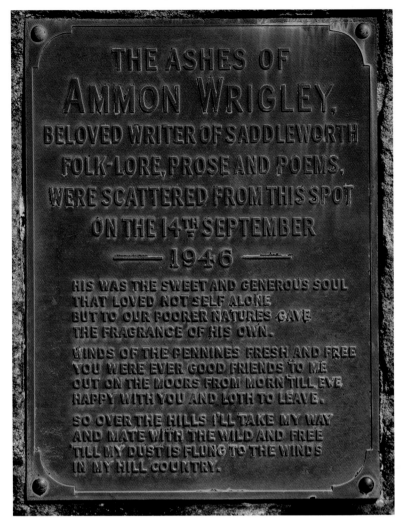

Memorial to Ammon Wrigley on Dinner Stone Rock, Standedge.

Standedge Canal Tunnel

The Standedge Canal Tunnel is the highest (643ft/196m above sea level), longest (3¼ miles/5km) and deepest (636ft/194m) canal in the country. The project was started in 1794 at the height of the Canal Age and took seventeen years and the lives of fifty men to complete.

The first engineer was Benjamin Outram but he was succeeded by Thomas Telford in 1806 when it was realized that the two ends were at different heights and would not meet in the middle. Five reservoirs – Swellands, Black Moss, Redbrook, Diggle and March Haig – were needed to supply the canal with enough water.

The Standedge Tunnel and Visitor Centre at Tunnel End, Marsden is a great introduction to the Huddersfield Narrow Canal, the second canal built to link Yorkshire and Lancashire. The first was the Rochdale Canal. In the visitor centre, you can actually have a go at 'legging' through the tunnel, just like the old canal navigators did, and see how the canal was excavated through the stony heart of the Pennines.

The trip on a glass-roofed narrowboat into the mouth of the Standedge Tunnel is a real step back in time, as you wonder at the work which went into this major feat of eighteenth-century engineering. You have the choice of a thirty-minute excursion into the tunnel, or the more adventurous may like to consider the three-hour trip right through the tunnel all the way to Diggle on the other side of the hill. And if you are really fit, you might even like to consider the walk 'over the top' across Castleshaw Moor and Close Moss, using the Standedge Trail to get back to Standedge.

The first single-bore Standedge railway tunnel was constructed between 1845 and 1849 by the Huddersfield and Manchester Railway Company and alongside the canal tunnel, which was used to remove spoil from the excavations. It was the longest in the world at the time at 3 miles, 66 yards. A second tunnel was constructed between 1868 and 1871, and a third, double-track tunnel between 1890 and 1894, which is still in use by the Trans-Pennine Express.

A plaque set into a boulder at Dinner Stone Rock commemorates the much-loved dialect author and poet Ammon Wrigley (1861–1946), who gained a huge following in the district of his native Saddleworth. He loved these hills, and an annual ceremony in his honour is still held here by the Ammon Wrigley Society. His poem 'On the Stanedge Moors' could have been written about a spot just like this:

When the Stanedge moors are August brown,
Away to the heights I go,
Up old hill roads where the ruts are deep,
To a hollow that few men know.
And there I lie in the windblown grass,
Away from a world of strife;
And I take mine ease where all things go
In the simple ways of life.

A restored path leads you on to the next major landmark on the Way, and you'll have been hearing it as a dull roar for some time before you actually see it. The angry buzz of the M62 trans-Pennine motorway at Windy Hill is crossed by an elegant footbridge which, although an obvious modern intrusion into the moorland world, is actually a thing of quite startling beauty. For the motorists passing beneath it in the head-long rush of motorway madness, its white concrete spars look like mirror images of the old BOAC logo. It says something about the importance of the Way that it had to be constructed especially and at enormous expense to carry what is, after all, merely a footpath across the motorway.

Defoe's 'Andes' lie ahead, as you blithely stride now dry-footed along the paved track crossing the aptly named Slippery Moss and

Redmires, once one of the boggiest, most unpleasant parts of the route. Blackstone Edge (1,550ft/472m) is a typical South Pennine escarpment of gritstone, overlooking the glinting waters of Hollingworth Lake and the milltowns of West Lancashire. But it is most famous for the so-called 'Roman Road' still marked on some maps, which crosses its northern end.

The beautifully paved and graded roadway is actually a double-width packhorse causeway track, and documentary evidence shows that it was widened as a turnpike between Littleborough and Ripponden in 1734. It may well have followed the route of a former Roman road which linked their forts at Littleborough and Aldborough, but the idea that the central drainage channel was worn by the brake poles of Roman chariots is stretching belief a bit too far.

An ancient boundary marker known as the Aiggin Stone, which may have been named after the Saxon god Aigle, stands where the Way crosses the causey track. Most probably it was a marker at the highest point of the pass which marks the tribal border between Lancashire and Yorkshire.

The gritstone exclamation mark of the monument on the summit of Stoodley Pike – a tantalizing, beckoning goal as you skirt the reservoirs on Light Hazzles Edge – is the next highlight along the route. There is something about these South Pennine hills which seem to attract monument builders, as most milltowns seem to have one or two punctuating their horizons like ever-constant old friends.

The Stoodley Pike monument was originally built in 1814 to commemorate the abdication of Napoleon and the Peace of Ghent, but when Napoleon escaped from Elba in 1815, work was postponed until after Wellington's victory at the Battle of Waterloo later that

The Pennine Way footbridge crossing the M62 motorway.

The so-called 'Roman Road' on Blackstone Edge.

year had finally laid the ghost of old Boney. In 1854 the monument collapsed and the present, blunt, soot-blackened obelisk which stands about 125ft/38m high was constructed two years later.

As you make the wooded descent into the Calder valley to cross the Rochdale Canal at Mytholm, it's all meadows and rough pasture. But we have not left the gritstone moors behind quite yet because the next highlight is Top Withins, the bleak moorland setting for *Wuthering Heights* above Haworth and at the romantic heart of Brontë country.

Emily Brontë explained that the name of Heathcliff's house at Wuthering Heights was derived from 'wuthering' or 'withering' – the highly appropriate local word to describe the typical Pennine weather. The 'ventilation' up here was, she wrote, 'pure and bracing' and could be judged 'by the excessive slant of a few stunted firs at the end of the house; and by a range of gaunt thorns all stretching their limbs one way, as if craving alms of the sun. Happily, the architect had foresight to build it strong: the narrow windows are deeply set in the wall, and the corners defended with large, jutting stones.'

It is unlikely that the truncated and roofless ruined farmhouse that is Top Withins was really Emily's model for her hero's home. The plaque on the wall erected by the Brontë Society honestly claims that, even when complete, the farmhouse bore no resemblance to the house she described. But the situation certainly matches Heathcliff's house, and the clumps of sycamores by the house are often bent in the constant, 'wuthering' winds, like those firs and thorns which surrounded the fictional Wuthering Heights.

More long miles across moors haunted by grouse and curlew follow, as the route eventually passes through the villages of Ickornshaw and Lothersdale and then into Gargrave and the valley of the River Aire. Following the source of the river at Aire Head Springs, you enter Malham and an entirely different world.

Malham, it has to be said, can be a bit of a shock to the system after all those moorland miles of strenuous bogtrotting. At long last you've left behind the grimy, soot-blackened milltowns, ruinous farmsteads and broken-down gritstone walls of the Peak, the South Pennines and Calderdale. Ahead lie the sweet pastures, springy turf and more pastoral scenes as you enter Craven country, and the Carboniferous limestone of the Yorkshire Dales. Many Wayfarers have been heard to breathe a deep sigh of relief.

Anglophile and former Dales resident Bill Bryson thought Malhamdale was heaven on earth. He once wrote: 'I won't know for sure if Malhamdale is the finest place there is until I have died and seen heaven (assuming they let me at least have a glance), but until that day comes, it will certainly do.'

Of course, the great scenic attraction of Malham is its magnificent Cove, and neighbouring Gordale Scar. The awesome 300ft/90m amphitheatre of the Cove once echoed to a thunderous waterfall higher even than Niagara when Ice Age meltwaters crashed over its lip 10,000 years ago. Today its vertiginous terraces are the haunt of ravens and rock climbers, and Pennine Wayfarers have a birds's eye view of their activities as they climb the rocky staircase which ascends the western side of the sweeping rock face.

On top of the cove, you encounter the first limestone pavement met on the Way. The fretted jigsaw landscape of clints (blocks) and grykes (crevices) has to be negotiated to get the stunning view down Airedale from the lip of the cove. In the right light of early morning or late afternoon, you'll be able to pick out the shadowy shelves of lynchets (Iron Age cultivation terraces) which line the green slopes of Shorkley Hill.

Apparently, Malham receives as many visitors as Uluru (formerly Ayers Rock), in the Australian outback, so after your endless miles of solitary walking it can come be a relief to head away from the crowds and up the dramatic dry canyon of Watlowes. After crossing Prior Rakes you reach the next scenic highlight, the oddity of Malham Tarn – a natural lake sited incongruously in the middle of porous limestone country. A bed of impervious shale provides the reason for this strange accident of nature; it is one of very few large natural sheets of water you will come across on your Pennine journey.

Gordale Scar

Both wonders of Malhamdale – Malham Cove and the neighbouring Gordale Scar to the east – mark the line of the Middle Craven Fault, a major fracture in the Great Scar limestone running east to west across the landscape of the Yorkshire Dales. The final polish on these dramatic landscapes was administered by glacial action during the last Ice Age, and the scouring action of icy glacial meltwater.

The Gothic atmosphere of Gordale Scar has attracted the attention of poets and painters from Thomas Gray to J.M.W. Turner and James Ward, whose masterpiece of the Scar dwarfing a miniscule White Park bull now hangs in London's Tate Gallery. The 300-foot overhanging walls of limestone enclose Gordale Beck, which issues from the living rock at its very heart in a double waterfall, invisible to the walker until the very last minute.

There's an entertaining little scramble up the left of the lower falls which leads under the upper one, where the water spouts clear from a hole in the wall of the gorge. It's one of the most dramatic scenes in the Pennines.

Two walkers – and a dog – stroll along the dry valley of Watlowes, surrounded by limestone scars and pavements.

Despite its early description as a 'mountain marathon', the Pennine Way crosses very few real mountain peaks. But summit-baggers have a treat ahead in the noble, stepped profile of Pen-y-Ghent (2,273ft/696m), the 'hill of the winds' and the lowest of Yorkshire's famous Three Peaks.

The Way ascends Pen-y-Ghent after contouring around Fountains Fell (named after its original owners, the great Cistercian abbey in far-off Nidderdale) from Dale Head, joining the popular path from Brackenbottom. It is steep at the start, but restoration work on the path makes it much easier than it used to be, and you are soon clambering

through the rock steps of alternating gritstone and shale to reach the summit. It you are lucky enough to be here in April, you'll find the limestone cliffs of Pen-y-Ghent awash with colour as the blooms of purple saxifrage tumble in glorious profusion from the ledges.

The descent from Pen-y-Ghent takes you down a walled, green lane past the impressive open pothole of Hull Pot over to the right and down into the village of Horton-in-Ribblesdale, where the drunken arches in the nave of the parish church of St Oswald should not be blamed on an unwise visit to the Crown Hotel. Horton is the centre of Three Peak Country, and the starting and finishing point for most people on the 26-mile, 12-hour marathon is usually the Pen-y-Ghent Café.

More potholes await as you stride out of Horton up another walled lane which passes Sell Gill Holes, Jackdaw Hole, Long Churn and Calf Holes, evil-looking fissures in the limestone which attract that most esoteric of outdoor folk, the potholers. They can can often be seen equipped with ropes, head-torches, mucky overalls, and a steely look of masochistic determination on their faces.

Your eyes, however, will be set on the next major objective on the Way, and that is the pretty little upper Wensleydale market town of Hawes, set in the valley of the River Ure. Hawes is perhaps most famous as the home of Wensleydale cheese, a crumbly local delicacy made in a creamery which was only saved from closure by vociferous local support.

Near by in the tiny hamlet of Hardraw, the spectacular sight of England's highest single-drop waterfall – the 100ft/30m vertical chute of Hardraw Force – awaits on payment of a small entrance fee at the

Ribblehead Viaduct

Seen from the summit of Whernside, the highest of Yorkshire's Three Peaks, the filigree, lace-like structure of the Ribblehead Viaduct seems to emphasize the fragility and impermanence of Man's presence in this wild landscape.

The sweeping, 24-arch Batty Moss viaduct is the iconic highlight on the 72-mile/116km Settle–Carlisle railway – 'the line that refused to die.' Threatened with closure since the days of the infamous Dr Beeching, an army of volunteers fought to keep the scenic line open – and against all the odds, they succeeded.

The remaining 325 bridges, 21 viaducts, 14 tunnels and 21 stations are a monument to the 2,000 navvies and their families who built it between 1869–76, living in appalling conditions in a shanty town known as Batty Green at Ribblehead.

Gaping Gill

The Bank Holiday descent by bosun's chair into the depths of Gaping Gill is the only way mere mortals can get a glimpse of the usually unseen world of the potholer. Arranged by local caving clubs, the vertiginous descent into the 340ft/104m deep shaft where Fell Beck disappears as it flows off the south side of Ingleborough is a thrilling experience.

Gaping Gill, for long thought to hold the longest waterfall, deepest shaft and largest cave chamber in Britain, is thought to be big enough to swallow York Minster. To stand in the echoing main chamber and watch the water spill down from the diverted beck above is a view of the Dales you will never forget. The first descent was made by the French pioneer caver Edouard Martel in 1895 and, since then, cavers have discovered more than 9 miles/15km of passages through the limestone linking Gaping Gill and Ingleborough Cave, on the ascent of Ingleborough from Clapham.

A prophetic lintel in Hawes.

and 'keld', meaning a spring. The charming village of Thwaite was the birthplace of brothers Richard and Cherry Kearton, pioneers of nature photography.

Keld marks a special crossroads on the walkers' map of England, as it is exactly half way along Alfred Wainwright's Coast to Coast Walk, and the footbridge over the River Swale is where it crosses the Pennine Way. Kisdon Force, just off the route under Birk Hill, is the biggest and best-known of the many waterfalls in the upper reaches of the Swale, said to be the fastest-flowing English river. As the river emerges from a narrow gorge, it plunges 10 ft/3m into a large pool, and then cascades over three limestone terraces and into a narrow trough, where eddies form fascinating patterns in the whisky-brown water.

Now it's up and over Stonesdale Moor to the welcoming sight of the Tan Hill Inn, at 1,732ft/530m, the highest pub in England. Still the scene of an annual sheep sale in May, Tan Hill was actually built to serve the needs of a small but active coal mining industry, which started as early as the thirteenth century and only ceased in the 1930s. More recently, the Tan Hill was the subject of a famous double-glazing advert and the centre of an unlikely legal battle with the Kentucky Fried Chicken fast-food chain.

The pub had dared to use the innocuous words 'Family Feast' to advertise its Christmas dinners. KFC claimed that 'Family Feast' was their trademark – but justice was served, and the inevitable outcome was an even redder face for Colonel Sanders.

The track from Tan Hill leads down across the peaty wastes of Stainmore – here significantly known simply as The Bog and haunted by the mournful call of waders such as redshank, lapwing and golden

Bowes Castle.

Green Dragon pub. Occasional brass band concerts still take place nearby, when the oom-pah-pah of the tubas can be heard against the backdrop of the thundering falls. Tightrope artist Blondin once famously crossed the waterfall amphitheatre on a wire, only stopping halfway to cook an omelette.

Another mountain lies ahead as you climb effortlessly up over a restored path towards the beckoning cairn on top of Great Shunner Fell – at 2,330ft/713m, the highest point so far reached on the Way. This is a fine viewpoint on a good day, with views extending west to the Lake District, ahead into the deep gash of Swaledale, and back towards the Three Peaks.

The Way long leads down to Thwaite and Keld, in perhaps the wildest and most beautiful of the Yorkshire Dales – Swaledale. The names of both villages reflect their Norse ancestry – 'thwaite' translating to a clearing

plover – crossing the River Greta at God's Bridge. This is a remarkable though often overlooked natural arch of limestone, which has been used for centuries by men and their animals on the ancient drove way between Bowes and Brough.

The angry roar of traffic on another trans-Pennine highway, this time the A66, is another unfortunate and jarring intrusion, but the next few miles across Cotherstone Moor, passing beneath the strange, flat-topped outcrop known as Goldsborough, are among the oddest along the entire Way. This area was until fairly recently used by the Army for artillery training, but although most of the warning signs are gone now, there's still an eerie air about the place, especially around the former farmstead of Levy Pool.

The gritstone escarpment of Goldsborough – looking every bit like a marooned Peakland 'edge' or an Arizonan mesa stranded in the middle of the moor – was obviously of ritual importance to the earliest prehistoric settlers, because evidence of their rock shelters and enigmatic cup-and-ring marked stones have been discovered there.

Low Birk Hat farmstead, on the northern shores of the Blackton Reservoir in Baldersdale, was made famous as the home of the reclusive Daleswoman, Hannah Hauxwell, whose spartan, lonely life was recounted by Barry Cockcroft in *Too Long a Winter*, an award-winning television documentary first broadcast in 1973. Hannah finally left the farm in 1989 and now lives in the nearby village of Cotherstone. A lasting legacy however is Hannah's Meadow alongside the Way, now a Site of Special Scientific Interest administered by the Durham Wildlife Trust as a local nature reserve.

Pennine Way sign pointing to Goldsborough Rocks, Baldersdale.

On Crossthwaite Common you pass the mysterious, pine-topped Kirkcarrion tumulus. Local legends associate this strange, other-worldly place with ghost and murders. But the truth is that it is a 3,000-year-old Bronze Age burial mound, set high on this prominent hill so that the worthy dead could watch over the living toiling in the fields below.

Passing more reservoirs in the Lune valley, the Way now heads for the glories of Teesdale, finally arriving in the bustling township of Middleton-in-Teesdale. Middleton was the headquarters for the Quaker-owned London Lead Company, which exploited the surrounding fells for their deposits of galena (lead ore) during the nineteenth century, and was a major benefactor to the pleasant Teeside town.

The next few miles on the Pennine Way are among the most spectacular along the whole route, as you walk upstream along the flower-decked banks of the Tees. You pass several scenic highlights all created by the landshaping force of the Whin Sill, a hard, black dolerite intrusion which was forced up through the Carboniferous sediments. It created landmark features which range from the Farne Islands to the east, to the natural defensive wall on which Hadrian's Wall was constructed.

The first of these highlights is Low Force, a stepped, tumbling torrent over columnar joints of the Whin Sill just beyond Wynch Bridge, a swinging suspension bridge which is claimed to be the first in Europe and was originally constructed by lead miners in 1704. The present structure was built in 1830.

You'll soon be hearing the thunder of England's most powerful waterfall – the 70ft/21m high High Force, embowered among trees but always an impressive sight. The best view, it must be said, is from the opposite bank but for that you would have to pay an entrance fee to reach it from the adjacent High Force Hotel.

High Force may not be the highest waterfall in England, but it's certainly the most spectacular, especially when the peat-stained waters of the Tees have been swollen after heavy rain. No other British waterfall can match it for sheer power, and it's one of the few places passed on the Pennine Way which truly merits that over-used epithet of 'awesome'.

The Way now passes through a dwarf forest of stunted gin-scented junipers, but for botanists, the highlight comes as it enters the National Nature Reserve of Upper Teesdale. Here, in the right season, Ice Age relict species such as pink bird's eye primrose, Alpine cinquefoil, golden globeflower and the electric blue of spring gentian carpet the meadows of Widdybank and Cronkley Fell below Falcon Clints and the foaming cascade of Caldron Snout – now unfortunately tamed and regulated as an outflow from the vast and ultimately unnecessary Cow Green Reservoir above.

The Whin Sill intrusion on the underlying limestone created the granular rocks known as sugar limestone, providing a uniquely fertile habitat for the rare Ice Age flora of Upper Teesdale. A great, long-forgotten landscape feature which sadly disappeared under the bland, lapping waters of Cow Green was the celebrated 'Wheel of the Tees' – a vast, swinging meander in the riverbed.

The flowers of Upper Teesdale were incidental to John Wood, as he confessed in *Mountain Trail*, his delightful 1947 account of the proposed Pennine Way. He had fonder memories of 'the Weel' as he called it. 'For myself, I confess that on hot days I have been more interested in the possibilities of bathing in the Weel, which is an expanded and tranquil reach of the Tees with a five-foot depth of water for several hundred yards. One scorching August day I had the luck to be one of an all-male bathing party, and by going out of sight of the bridge round a bend we were able to indulge in the most enjoyable form of swimming and keep our costumes dry.'

As you cross the Tees above Cauldron Snout, you leave Durham and enter Cumbria, following Maize Beck towards what for many people is the greatest spectacle on the entire Pennine Way. Nothing quite prepares you for the jaw-dropping moment as you cross the final flat limestone outcrops and shake holes of High Cup Plain. You suddenly find yourself teetering on the edge of a yawning abyss, with a whole new world opening out out at your feet.

High Cup Nick – the name really only applies to the apex of the gorge on which you are standing – has been dubbed the Grand Canyon of the Pennines. This huge bite out of the western scarp of the range has also been called the most glorious landscape feature in northern England. The result of glacial action, the vast ampitheatre drops away beneath your feet, the tiny silver thread of High Cup Gill winding hundreds of feet below and the western views extending far out towards the misty Vale of Eden and the distant blue outline of the Lakeland hills. What a moment, and one which will make you forget all those thigh-aching, toe-blistering miles you have endured to reach this magical point.

A homesick W.H. Auden, exiled in New York during the Second World War, regarded this spot as 'one of the sacred places of the earth' and he described it in his 1940 poem, 'New Year Letter':

> There where the Eden leisures through
> Its sandstone valley, is my view
> Of green and civil life that dwells
> Below a cliff of savage fells

Around the rim of the ravine, columns of steely-grey dolerite create a grandstand palisade, and include the hard-to-find rocky finger known as Nichol's Chair or Last, 20 yards off the main path. It was named after a Dufton cobbler who had the audacity – and sheer nerve – to climb to its crumbling summit and sole and heel a pair of boots while sitting on the top. Apparently, no one thought to ask him why.

The route now descends on a pleasant path known as Narrow Gate into a walled lane which leads into the charming red sandstone village of Dufton, pleasingly grouped around its village green. As the ever-pragmatic Wainwright pointed out,

> it's slightly galling to note that your long-term objective of Kirk Yetholm is actually further way at the end of this glorious day than it was at the beginning. Thanks Alfred, but it was worth it.

The highest points on the Way now await, with the long, partly slabbed climb up from Dufton over Knock Fell, past the incongruous, white golf-ball radome-topped Great Dun Fell and finally gaining the crowning summit of the Pennines (and the Pennine Way) – the 2,930ft/893m Cross Fell.

A reminder that you are still very much on England's watershed is the humbling fact that a drop of rain landing on the boggy saddle just before you reach Cross Fell's summit could either end up heading west towards the Eden and the Solway Firth, or east towards the mighty Tees and eventually the North Sea.

Cross Fell is a fascinating mountain for many reasons. Geologically, it's a bit of an oddity because the traditional Pennine mix of gritstone and limestone to which we have become accustomed over many previous miles also includes intrusions of Whin Sill and various other minerals. Coal, silver and lead mines have been worked around its broad, windswept summit at various times, and the scars remain in the form of the abandoned remains of the former workings.

The only wind in Britain to have its own name is Cross Fell's famous Helm wind. It occurs when a north-easterly blows up and over the Pennines, tumbling sometimes with amazing force over the western escarpment of Cross Fell and creating a distinctive bar or bank of cloud.

Cross Fell was formerly known as Fiends' Fell and was said by local people in the Eden valley to be the haunt of devils. That was before the saintly Paulinus held a mass there some time in the seventh century, exorcising the demons and giving the fell its modern name. The only cross you'll find on the summit today is the huge drystone-walled windbreak east of the summit cairn.

John Wood claimed that the view from the summit cairn on Cross Fell on a rare clear day was the grandest one-way view in England. It extends north to the Solway Firth, Criffel and the Galloway Hills, and westwards across the Vale of Eden to Blencathra, Skiddaw and the other misty-blue Lakeland hills.

It's still a long and weary 4 miles down the old Corpse Road passing the remains of several lead mines and the bothie of Greg's Hut (named after climber John Gregory who died in the Alps in 1968) before you reach the welcome fleshpot of Garrigill, in the valley of the South Tyne, and the tree-shaded, riverside path to Alston.

Alston, close to the confluence of the River Net with the South Tyne, claims to be the highest market town in England – a statistic always disputed by Buxton in the Peak. Like Buxton, Alston's prosperity was founded on the lead found in the surrounding hills. It's been mined here along with silver, since medieval times.

The section of the Way between Alston and Greenhead is one of the least memorable on the entire route, following sections of the Roman Maiden Way as it crosses the great wilderness of Blenkinsopp Common. But it's a great place to spot birds of prey, such as buzzards, short-eared owls, and, if you are really lucky, peregrine falcons or goshawks.

The hamlet of Greenhead marks the start of the next great historical highlight of the Way – Hadrian's Wall. Built at the behest of Emperor Hadrian, in AD 120–8 to mark the northernmost limit of his empire, it acted as a barrier against the possible invasion by the heathen Caledonians from what we now know as Scotland. Current thinking is that the Wall was as much a political border as a defensive one.

It is a masterpiece of military engineering, and one of the finest examples of Roman military architecture anywhere in Europe, still impressive after nearly 2,000 years. It is amazing to think that it took the force of 10,000 professional legionaries (not slaves incidentally) only eight years to build, a feat which probably could not be matched by today's computer-aided civil engineers. With its series of turrets, milecastles, forts and the vallum – a sort of no-man's-land between the Wall and the military road, running parallel to the south – the Wall ran for 80 Roman miles (73 miles/117km) across the neck of England from the Tyne to the Solway. It is now a UNESCO World Heritage Site, and in the care of English Heritage.

The Roman engineers cleverly utilized the outcrop of volcanic Whin Sill rock for much of its length, placing it on top of the cliffs and giving it a natural defence against attack from the north. We'll witness this as we follow the legionaries along the Wall from Thirlwall Castle, a fourteenth century pele tower built largely from stones from the Wall, over Walltown, Cawfields and Whinshields Crags (the highest point, 1,132ft/345m, on the Wall, from which on a good day both the Solway Firth and North Sea can be seen) to Peel Crags and Crag Lough (probably the finest viewpoint) and Hotbank Crags, leaving the Wall to head north again at Rapishaw Gap.

Skirting Broomlea Lough, the coniferous gloom of the Wark Forest looms ahead. The next few miles are probably the least attractive of any section of the Way as it plunges through the monotonous Sitka spruce

An empty and abandoned quarry house on Alston Moor.

Vindolanda

When archaeologist Robin Birley first discovered faint scratchings on scraps of wood made by a Roman stylus he unearthed from a wet drainage pit at the settlement of Vindolanda, south of Hardian's Wall in 1973, he could have no idea of their importance.

The tablets were preserved because they had been dumped into a wet ditch, where the anaerobic conditions did not allow them to rot. The messages were written in ink onto so-called 'leaf' tablets, made of imported spruce or larch.

Writing tablets are still being unearthed at Vindolanda and most are now kept in the British Museum in London. After years of patient excavation, restoration and then interpretation, we have discovered much about what life on the Wall was like for the soldiers and their families, nearly 2000 years ago: from what they ate and drank, what they wore, to what they thought of some of their senior colleagues and their own family and friends.

forestry plantations which cloak so much of Northumberland under their regimented green bottle brushes.

A slight detour off the Way north of Bellingham (pronounced 'Belling-jum' by the way), is the delightful cascade of Hareshaw Linn, at the head of a pretty wooded dene – as steep valleys are known hereabouts. It's well worth the mile or so to see it, because there are few other highlights between here and Redesdale.

The long climb out of Bellingham will take you over the charmingly named Deer Play, Whitley Pike and Padon Hill, crowned by its 1920s pepperpot summit cairn. If you are lucky enough to be here in August or September, you'll be treated to some of the finest displays of heather moorland in Northumberland. Then it's back to the gloomy rides of the Border Forest again, all the way down into Bryness.

There's more forestry on the Way out of Bryness, but a welcome break will bring you to the grassy playing-card square ramparts of the Roman Chew Green marching camp just beyond Ogre Hill, with a signal station on Brownhart Law above. Superimposed on the mounds of Chew Green is the deserted medieval village of Kemylpethe, proving that although these windy heights are largely unpeopled now, they were once much more densely populated.

The Cheviots which face you now are the final great challenge on the Pennine Way, and they represent some of the toughest walking to be found on the trail. The reason for this lies in their geology. The Cheviots are the eroded remains of a great granite boss formed when a huge volcano, situated just to the west of the 2,676ft (815m) summit of the reigning peak of The Cheviot, spewed out its lava about 300 million years ago. Several thousands of feet thick, the lava gives the pinkish hue to the grey granites, which are rarely exposed in crags except in places like the Hen Hole and The Schil in the remote College valley.

Clennel Street, an old drovers' road near Alwinton.

Granite is impervious to water and so the one outstanding feature that the walker finds when crossing the Cheviots is peat bog – cloying, ankle-sucking peat bog – which makes progress extremely difficult. However, the National Park has created sandstone flagged paths through many of the most difficult stretches of mire across the Cheviots – largely to keep walkers from eroding this internationally rare habitat.

Having said that, this next part of the Way was always Tom Stephenson's favourite, and he plumped for the 2,034ft/620m Windy Gyle as his number one location on the entire route. 'Looking over that great expanse . . . those great rounded hills and deep winding valleys and the play of light over them, I think probably I would plump for the Cheviots as my favourite ground,' he revealed.

And it's true that the constantly windswept, open moorland of the Cheviots can give you an unparalleled sense of freedom and being on top of the world. There's always the brooding, unseen threat of danger in the air, so often felt in border country. You half expect a band of steel-bonneted reivers to come charging up the hillsides of Ravens Knowe, Coquet Head, Lamb Hill or Mozie Law, as the path follows the ramshackle post and wire fence which is the undistinguished boundary between England and Scotland for several miles.

The great Northumbrian historian Professor G.M. Trevelyan, perhaps encapsulated it best in his book *The Middle Marches*. He wrote: 'In Northumberland alone, both heaven and earth are seen, we walk all day on long ridges, high enough to give far views of moor and valley, and the sense of solitude below. It is the land of far horizons.'

Your next horizon is the 2,674ft/815m summit of The Cheviot itself, but this hour-long detour is only for the determined summit-bagger and completist, because the sticky going across the peat bogs, now largely paved it has to be said, will serve as an unpleasant reminder of those early days on Kinder Scout, Bleaklow and Black Hill at the start of your marathon.

The main route from Windy Gyle contours high above the beautiful and isolated College valley crossing Kings Seat and Auchope Cairn to the pass of Red Cribs, with its welcome reconstructed refuge hut, and then up and over the splintered andesite summit of The Schil (1,985ft/605m), the last real hill on the Way and many people's favourite Cheviot summit. The views across the valley are superb from here; to the deep and menacing hanging valley known as the Hen Hole, and eastward down the valley towards the coastal plain and distant North Sea.

The end is in sight now, as you follow the Halter Burn (note the Scottish name) down off the Cheviots. A final stretch of road walking will take you into Kirk Yetholm and your long-awaited destination. Before the village became the northern terminus of the Pennine Way, the green

Rock Art

Strange and intricate patterns of cups, concentric rings, channels and spirals have been carved on many prominent boulders which overlook wide areas of the Northumberland countryside. They represent the finest collection of prehistoric cup-and-ring marked rocks in Britain.

Archaeologists still argue about what they represent: theories range from messages from outer space to ancient representations of the landscape, but no one can be really sure. But they must have carried some kind of message about the landscape and what it meant 5,000 years ago.

Among the best places to see rock art and cup-and-ring marks in Northumberland is at Lordenshaws, near Rothbury; Roughting Linn, near Ford, and on the Iron Age hill-fort at Old Berwick. But they can also be found on Gardom's Edge in the Peak District, on Ilkley Moor in lower Wharfedale, and at Goldsborough on Cotherstone Moor.

around which Kirk Yetholm clusters was most famous as a popular gypsy encampment. Esther Faa Blythe, the last Gypsy Queen, died at this Mecca for Romanies in 1883, and Sir Walter Scott is said to have based his character Meg Merrilies on a former resident of Kirk Yetholm.

The mock-Tudor Border Hotel at Kirk Yetholm is the official end of the Way, and Alfred Wainwright's rather rash offer (which he later regretted – it cost him an estimated £15,000 between 1968 and his death in 1991) of a free half-pint at the bar for those who have completed the marathon, still applies, provided certain conditions are fulfilled.

Black Midden Bastle House, near Bellingham.

CONCLUSION

Tom Stephenson's concept of a walk along the length of upland England was, as we have seen, his way of bringing pressure on Government and landowners for the opening up of the forbidden moorlands, particularly in the Peak District.

But it owed its inspiration to the Appalachian Trail in America, and the idea of a continuous walk along a watershed range has an abiding appeal to ramblers, whatever their ability and experience. So it has proved with the Pennine Way, still the most popular and best-known of the National Trails.

The unbridled enthusiasm of the virgin Pennine Wayfarer can be gauged from John Wood's stirring call to arms in his wonderful *Mountain Trail: The Pennine Way from the Peak to the Cheviots* of 1947, a book which is illustrated by Donald Foster's immaculate pen and ink drawings.

A pilgrimage is proclaimed! Let us resolve upon tramping to Scotland by high ways that avoid highways, keeping as much as we can over the thousand-foot contour, and climbing above two thousand whenever possible. Anyone with a few pounds in his purse can pay for a railway ticket to Carlisle or Berwick and beyond, or can fill the petrol tank of his car or motor-cycle and see the hundreds of advertisement hoardings on the main roads to the Border – but see precious little else. For ourselves, let us go where stout hearts, sturdy limbs and hardened feet are needed, and pioneer a trail that for long stretches is not even a dotted footpath-line on the one-inch map.

Sixty years of wear and tear caused by the feet of Wood's grateful pilgrims has meant that Stephenson's dream of a 'faint line' is nothing but a fond and distant memory, and the Pennine Way is now an unmistakeable green-dashed and lozenged line marching north across the OS maps.

But the romance of the route up England's backbone has attracted an enormous cross-section of walkers. Some of them have been famous in their own right, such as members of the cast of the long-running TV soap *Coronation Street* and celebrity charity fund-raisers like Sir Jimmy Saville, while others have been ordinary walkers of all ages who just enjoy the challenge of walking the watershed of England, often for charity.

One of the lesser-known Pennine Wayfarers was the controversial but brilliant football club manager Brian Clough, the subject of David Peace's hard-hitting novel *The Damned Utd* from 2006, and the subsequent critically acclaimed film.

'Old Big 'Ead' had just celebrated his club Nottingham Forest's return to the First Division in the summer of 1977 with a month's holiday in Majorca. When he got back, Clough undertook a week's walk along the southern half of the Pennine Way. Typically, he'd volunteered to support a party of Nottinghamshire miners who were raising money for the Royal Life Saving Society.

'You'll Never Walk Alone', Mick Davis's cartoon from *Peak Park News*, Summer, 1977

He wrote to the Peak District National Park office in Bakewell while I was an information assistant there, asking if we could provide him with a copy of Wainwright's *Pennine Way Companion*. Being an avid football fan myself, I was delighted to oblige.

The party set out on 13 June, accompanied by the club's doctor, Michael Hutson. Clough is reported to have joked: 'He's just doing it to look after my blisters!' Knowing Clough's steely determination, I'm sure he completed the route, and he might just have been amused by the many other 'cloughs' he was to meet along the Way.

As the editor of the Park's journal, *Peak Park News*, I couldn't resist asking my cartoonist friend, Mick Davis, to come up with an appropriate illustration to the story, which was captioned 'Keep right on to the end of the road,' for the end column on the back page.

Landscape photographer and guidebook author Walter Poucher's *The Backbone of England* was published in 1946. In it he devoted a whole section to the long battle for access to mountain and moorland, and to Tom Stephenson's proposal for a Pennine Way long distance path between Edale in the Peak and Wooler (eventually it was to be Kirk Yetholm) in Northumberland.

And he accurately described the reason behind the creation of the route: 'It is . . . well known that much of the moorland in the Derbyshire Peak is private ground: the notice boards which acquaint the pedestrian with this unfortunate fact are legion and confront him at almost every turn in the high ground.'

In the Pennines, said Poucher, the paths were few and far between and covered only a small part of the high ground. 'Anyone who doubts this state of affairs should try to amble on Kinderscout, a bare peaty plateau of some thirteen square miles which is uncrossed by a single right of way. He will be lucky if he is not accosted by a keeper and turned back off the moor.'

He concluded that the realization of Stephenson's dream would be 'a worthy tribute to those of our fighting men who love the hills, and the many beauty spots of our island heritage'. It would be another nineteen years before Stephenson's 'long green trail' would become the first official long distance footpath in Britain.

Another guidebook author who paid tribute to Tom Stephenson's vision was Alfred Wainwright, in his best-selling *Pennine Way Companion*, first published in 1968. The route was, he said:

the happy inspiration, some thirty years ago, of Mr Tom Stephenson, the present secretary of the Ramblers' Association; but he did more than think of the idea: he worked hard to bring it into being.

Many were the difficulties, and many were the objections, but all were overcome in a long and tedious campaign before Parliament set the seal of authority on a recommendation by the National Parks Commission and gave approval for this first long-distance right of way for walkers.

Officially, Whitehall created the Pennine Way. But those who walk it should remember that it was one man who inspired, in his mind and by his patience and effort, the freedom they enjoy. Mr Stephenson has served the cause of walkers well throughout a long life, but his name will most be revered for his imaginative conception of a continuous way for travellers on foot across half of England.

But Wainwright, just like Stephenson, never actually completed the route in 'one fell sweep' as Wainwright rather aptly described it. Both pioneers did it in easily manageable sections and the preliminary fieldwork and detailed notes for Wainwright's guide were actually done by four of his friends, 'good men and true', between 1966 and 1967. For the record, they were Harry Appleyard of Wigton (Tan Hill to Cross Fell); Len Chadwick of Dobcross (Edale to the Calder valley); Cyril Moore of Morecambe (Malham Tarn to Tan Hill), and Lawrence Smith of Deepcar (Calder valley to Malham Tarn).

Amblers, Ramblers and Scramblers

Pennine Way users are categorized in several different ways by Natural England, the government agency charged with its management. In its Pennine Way User Survey, undertaken in the summer of 2007, users were asked firstly whether they were short-distance users or dedicated National Trail users – that is, setting out to complete the whole Trail either in one go or over a series of visits. Then the short-distance users were spilt into a three further amusingly titled categories. They were either:

Amblers – who were out on the trail for less than an hour;
Ramblers – who were out for between one and four hours, or
Scramblers – who were out for a full day.

This categorization apparently enables NE to explore the different needs of different types of users. In the survey, 6 per cent were ramblers, 44 per cent scramblers and 33 per cent were regular National Trail users. Overall, 98 per cent of all users described their overall experience of the Pennine Way as 'very good' or 'fairly good'.

A quarter of those interviewed were aged between 45–54, and 23 per cent between 55 and 64 (which seems to indicate an aging constituency), and most came either with friends or family, as a couple or with a partner.

Of the 252 total responses to the survey (195 were by face-to-face interviews and 57 were responses on the web), a rather surprising 82 per cent claimed that 'nothing' had spoilt their visit. Four-by-four vehicles and motorbikes were the most annoying thing for Wayfarers at 22 per cent, closely followed by the poor walking surface. But among the specific responses was one which claimed the slabs were wonderful, and another praised the good clear paths and signage.

Most people (79 per cent) had travelled 20 miles or more to reach the trail, and the vast majority (62 per cent) travelled by car. What made them want to do it? The majority (34 per cent) said it was 'for the love of nature and landscape, including heritage', and only 11 per cent 'because it was a National Trail'.

The Future

What then is the future of Tom Stephenson's 'long green trail'? Steve Westwood, the Pennine Way National Trail Officer, believes that the level of use has declined over the years. 'A figure of 10,000 walkers a year used to be commonly given as the number of people who did the Pennine Way, but I haven't found any evidence for these kind of numbers. The figure is probably more like 1,800 to 2,000 a year today.'

There are numerous reasons for the decline, including the time people have available to do the entire route – although people seem to be willing to go to Nepal for a month's trekking – and competition from other National Trails and long distance routes. Our user surveys seems to indicate that more people seem to be doing the route in sections, at weekends for example, rather than the whole thing in one go. I wonder whether the recession will actually increase use, as people have more time on their hands.

The budget for maintainance work on the trail now stands at around £250,000 per annum, but despite the impression that some people might have, Steve reckons that less than 3 per cent of the total length is paved. 'This sort of improvement work will continue in places like the Cheviot ridge, where the original boardwalks, which did a good job, will need replacing by slabs,' explained Steve.

So I think the Pennine Way will be around for many more years, and the quality of the walking experience should improve. We are only now beginning to realize the importance of our peat moors as carbon reserves and for their ability to retain water and avert flooding further

downstream, so various stewardship schemes and projects like Moors for the Future will ensure the overall experience continues to be enhanced.

And what would Tom Stephenson think of all these management plans, user surveys and performance indicators? I think he'd just give one of his impish grins and say, in that warm Lancastrian burr, 'Aye, I'm just glad folk are out there and enjoying it.'

It may not be called Stephenson's Way – and that's the last thing he would have wanted – but for the serious long distance walker in this overcrowded little island, the Pennine Way will always be the greatest physical challenge, and the finest badge of honour.

Journey's end: entering Kirk Yetholm.

THE PHOTOGRAPHS

Beyond the fertile Edale valley, Grindslow Knoll rises up to the plateau of Kinder Scout.

The Pennine Way now goes via Upper Booth and Jacob's Ladder: the former 'bad weather' alternative.

LEFT The Anvil Stone, a distinctive landmark overlooking Grindsbrook.

BELOW The Boxing Gloves: one of the many eroded gritstone formations along the northern edge of the Kinder plateau.

RIGHT Noe Stool, shaped by water, wind and weather, with Swine's Back Rocks in the distance.

FAR RIGHT Looking down from Kinder towards the River Ashop and Ashop Head.

RIGHT BELOW The Wainstones: an old gritstone couple pucker up on the top of Bleaklow. (The alternative name for the formation, apparently coined by Wainwright, is 'The Kiss.')

Laddow Rocks, a prominent gritstone landmark in the Crowden valley.

Digley Reservoir, backed up by Black Hill and the TV mast of Holme Moss.

The reservoirs of Longdendale, with the Pennine Way rising through heather moorland towards Black Hill.

The view from Standedge into East Lancashire.

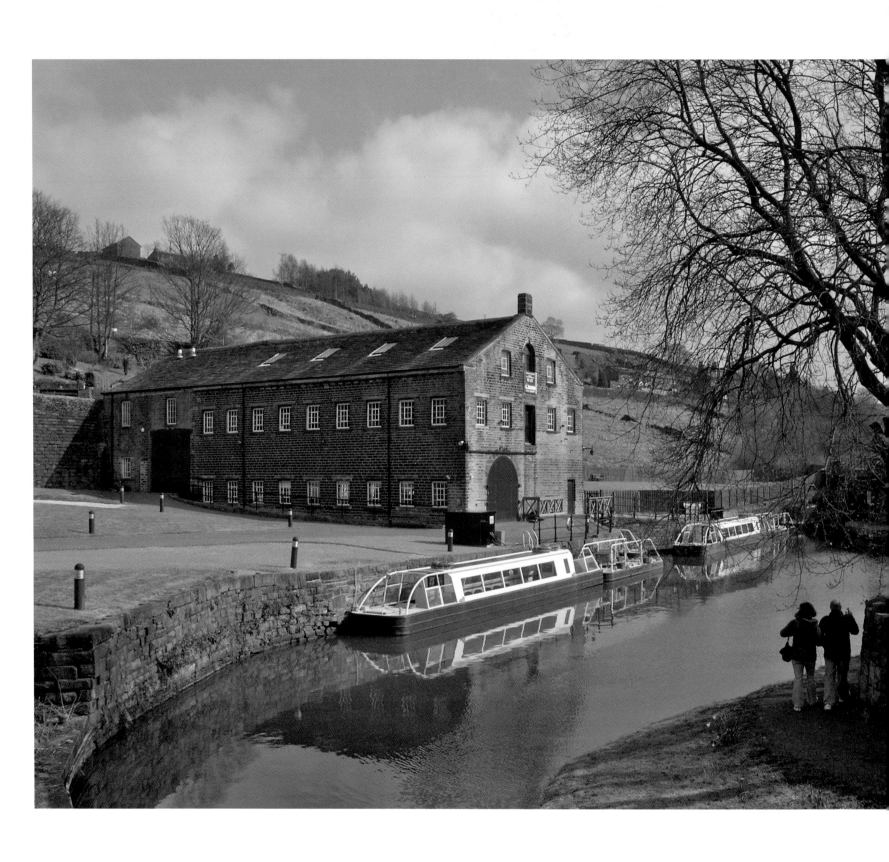

LEFT The Huddersfield Narrow Canal, near Marsden, which runs for 3½ miles/56km in the longest, highest and deepest canal tunnel in Britain beneath the Pennines between Marsden and Diggle.

ABOVE Buckstones, overlooking Standedge, is a popular place to fly radio-controlled gliders.

A mountain biker stops
to enjoy the view from
the rocky escarpment of
Blackstone Edge.

The view from Blackstone Edge, looking towards Hollingworth Lake and the mill towns of East Lancashire.

The Aiggin Stone, a guide
stone which for centuries
guided travellers across the
rough terrain of Blackstone
Edge.

Stoodley Pike, originally built to commemorate victory over Napoleon, viewed from Langfield Common.

Stone causeways are a fascinating
feature of the South Pennines; this
particularly fine example descends to
the youth hostel at Mankinholes.

LEFT Many stone causeways lead to chapels; this is the Methodist Chapel at Lumbutts.

BELOW The Calderdale valley, rising from farmland to unenclosed moorland and the prominence of Stoodley Pike.

When the valley bottoms were mostly
marshland, the roads in Calderdale kept to
higher ground.

ABOVE 'Top and bottom' houses – one dwelling built on top of another – rise steeply up the hillsides surrounding Hebden Bridge.

RIGHT Early morning on the Rochdale Canal as it passes through the gritstone mill town of Hebden Bridge.

OPPOSITE ABOVE The hill village of Heptonstall: a centre for the textile trades in pre-industrial times.

OPPOSITE BELOW LEFT A datestone in Heptonstall, featuring the likenesses of local innkeepers, Henry and Elizabeth Foster, as they would have looked in 1736.

OPPOSITE BELOW RIGHT Headstones at the chapel of Blackshaw Head, a small community overlooking the Colden valley.

49

Top Withins, on Haworth
Moor: the inspiration –
possibly – for Wuthering
Heights, in Emily Brontë's
novel.

Anyone who thinks
that West Yorkshire is
essentially urban should
follow the Pennine Way
across Haworth Moor.

ABOVE The churchyard, next to the Brontë parsonage, is claustrophobically full of gravestones and memorials.

RIGHT The steep main street of Haworth, still cobbled, heading down into the Worth valley.

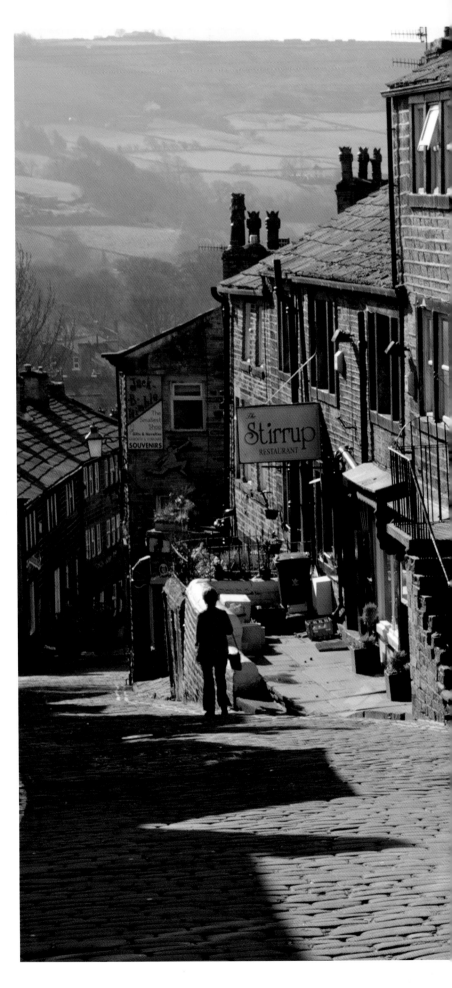

Wainman's Pinnacle,
overlooking the Aire valley:
another monument, built
in 1816, which celebrated
Wellington's victory at
Waterloo.

Sharing Earl Crag with
Wainman's Pinnacle is
Lund's Tower, a distinctive
folly.

LEFT The way things used to be, before GPS and Satnav: a milestone near Thornton-in-Craven.

BELOW A busy scene at a lock on the Leeds and Liverpool Canal, between Barnoldswick and East Marton.

RIGHT The bridge over the River Aire, at Gargrave, one of the few villages directly on the line of the Pennine Way.

BELOW A narrowboat glides past the old lock-keeper's cottage on the Leeds and Liverpool Canal, near Gargrave.

A typical landscape around
Malham: a field barn,
surrounded by limestone
scars and drystone walls.

LEFT Malham and Malham Beck, where the limestone Dales begin.

BELOW Above Malham the paths are easy to follow, through sheep-cropped grass.

ABOVE Malham Cove, one
of the Pennine Way's most
spectacular and iconic
landforms.

RIGHT The view from the top
of Malham Cove, revealing the
pattern of old field systems.

LEFT Janet's Foss, a diminutive waterfall near Gordale Scar.

BELOW Malham Tarn: one of the few opportunities for Pennine Wayfarers to watch the sun set over water.

RIGHT The distinctive profile of Pen-y-ghent announces that walkers have reached 'Three Peaks' country.

BELOW Pen-y-ghent provides a backdrop to the limestone scars and outcrops.

LEFT The way down from the lower slopes of Pen-y-ghent.

BELOW Another distinctive profile – Ingleborough – and a procession of vintage tractors.

FAR LEFT Tagged and inquisitive, a couple of bullocks graze on Cam Fell.

LEFT The Pennine Way follows a good track from Cam Fell down into Wensleydale.

LEFT BELOW Designed in 1784 for cotton spinning, Gayle Mill and its waterwheel were powered by water from Gayle Beck.

RIGHT Bealer Bank, a paved path, kept the parishioners of Hawes dry-shod as they walked to church on Sunday.

LEFT The market town of Hawes gives walkers the chance to stock up on provisions, and maybe enjoy a pint outside the White Hart.

BELOW Field barns and drystone walls characterize the glaciated U-shaped valley of Wensleydale.

RIGHT The lambs are half-grown even before the trees have burst into leaf.

LEFT Hardraw Force, the highest above ground single-drop waterfall in the country.

ABOVE Cotter Force: not as well-known as Hardraw, but still a dramatic sight after rain.

LEFT From this cairn on the flank of Stag's Fell, a walker (generally found on the other side of the camera) enjoys the view down into Wensleydale.

TOP From Great Shunner Fell the Pennine Way drops down into Swaledale and the tiny village of Thwaite.

ABOVE A short detour from the route finds the village of Muker: not much bigger than Thwaite, but with a pub.

This barn, framed by the flank of Kisdon Hill, must be one of the most photographed in the Yorkshire Dales.

The chapel in Keld, yet another tiny village and the last one in Upper Swaledale.

ABOVE 'Keld' means a spring; this is one of a number of attractive waterfalls near by.

OVERLEAF A strong candidate for the best view in the Dales: looking down Swaledale from the ruins of Crackpot Hall.

ABOVE Storm clouds gather over Crackpot Hall, backed up by spoil heaps from the former lead mines.

LEFT A track meanders down to a field barn, on the flank of Stonesdale Moor.

RIGHT Tan Hill Inn, the highest pub in the land, has long been a welcome sight for weary travellers.

LEFT Looking north from Tan Hill, across the featureless terrain of Sleightholme Moor.

BELOW Goldsborough Rocks, a prominent landmark on Cotherstone Moor.

LEFT A typical farmhouse in Baldersdale, built to withstand the worst of the Pennine weather.

BELOW Baldersdale, where Hannah Hauxwell lived a frugal existence at her farm, Low Birk Hat.

RIGHT Baldersdale and Hury Reservoir, beneath stormy skies.

BELOW RIGHT The tumulus of Kirkcarrion, topped by pine trees, marks the burial place of a Bronze Age chieftain.

BELOW FAR RIGHT Sunlight catches a field barn, as the Pennine Way leaves Middleton-in-Teesdale and approaches the River Tees.

BELOW The riverside walk offers views of Low Force, a series of waterfalls.

RIGHT High Force, where the River Tees plunges more than 65 feet (20 m) over a whinstone precipice.

TOP An isolated farmstead, backed up by gloomy Pennine weather and Cronkley Scar.

ABOVE A cyclist enjoys a traffic-free road in Upper Teesdale.

The farms and field barns on the Raby estate in Upper Teesdale are typically painted white.

LEFT The River Tees, overlooked by the escarpment of Falcon Clints.

BELOW Cauldron Snout, a roaring torrent after heavy rain, draining water from Cow Green Reservoir into the Tees.

LEFT High Cup Nick, one of the most dramatic landforms along the Pennine Way.

ABOVE A couple of walkers take a breather before making the descent into Dufton.

LEFT The distinctive water fountain on the village green of Dufton, framed by the conical shape of Dufton Pike.

BELOW St Lawrence's Church, in Kirkland, lit up – for a few seconds – by the last rays of the sun.

RIGHT The radar station on top of Great Dun Fell, part of the air traffic control system.

BELOW Spring comes early to the Eden valley, though Cross Fell, behind, is still in winter's grip.

RIGHT The empty expanse of Alston Moor, looking back at Cross Fell.

BELOW A stone cairn marks the way north, from the top of Cross Fell across Alston Moor towards the lead-mining village of Garrigill.

ABOVE A quiet corner of Alston, claimed to be the highest market town in England.

LEFT Grey clouds gather round a farmhouse near Garrigill.

ABOVE Cawfield Quarry: once a source of building stone, now a peaceful lake.

RIGHT Milecastle 42 on Hadrian's Wall: a source of dressed stone in the 1,600 years since the Romans abandoned the most northerly part of their empire.

At Steel Rigg the wall climbs to the top of Peel Crags,
with Crag Lough in the distance.

One of the most-photographed trees along Hadrian's Wall, at Sycamore Gap.

LEFT North of Bellingham, the Pennine Way passes this elaborate cairn on top of Padon Hill.

BELOW Open country at Brownrigg Head; Pennine Wayfarers can walk all day here without seeing another walker.

LEFT Across a ladder stile, the path skirts the stands of conifer trees in Gibshiel Plantation.

BELOW Early morning light picks out the ramparts and ditches at Chew Green: evidence not just of one Roman camp, but a whole complex.

LEFT A reminder that the Pennine Way crosses the Otterburn military training area, with soldiers more in evidence than walkers.

BELOW Beyond Chew Green walkers leave the Northumberland National Park behind, and follow the England-Scotland border.

Sheep graze the open, rolling, unenclosed contours of the Cheviot Hills.

The last leg of the Pennine Way – the 28 miles from Byrness to Kirk Yetholm – is arguably the most challenging section of the walk.

ABOVE Farming and military vehicles co-exist in the Coquet valley.

RIGHT Waiting for a bite: an angler tries his luck in the River Coquet.

ABOVE Journey's End: the Border Hotel in the tranquil Scottish village of Kirk Yethom.

RIGHT Looking back on the Pennine hills from the arable land of the Scottish Borders.

Select Bibliography

Mountain Trail: The Pennine Way from the Peak to the Cheviots by John Wood (Allen and Unwin, 1947)

The Pennine Way by Kenneth Oldham (Dalesman Publishing, 1960)

The Pennine Way (pamphlet) by Tom Stephenson (Ramblers' Association, 1963)

A Guide to the Pennine Way by Christopher John Wright (Constable, 1967)

Pennine Way Companion by A. Wainwright (Westmorland Gazette, 1968)

The Shell Book of the Pennine Way by Michael Marriott (Queen Anne Press, 1968)

The Pennine Way by Tom Stephenson (HMSO, 1969)

Along the Pennine Way by J.H.B. Peel (David & Charles, 1972)

Tom Stephenson (pamphlet) (Ramblers' Association, 1976)

Wainwright on the Pennine Way by A. Wainwright, photographs by Derry Brabbs (Michael Joseph, 1985)

Forbidden Land: the Struggle for Access to Mountain and Moorland by Tom Stephenson, ed. Anne Holt (Manchester University Press, 1989)

Pennine Way North: Bowes to Kirk Yetholm by Tony Hopkins (Arum Press, 1989)

Pennine Way South: Edale to Bowes by Tony Hopkins (Arum Press, 1990)

Pennine Ways by John Gillham (Crowood Press, 1994)

Features of the Pennine Way (encapsulated leaflet) (Field Studies Council/Countryside Agency/English Nature, 2006)

Pennine Way by Edward de la Billière, Keith Carter and Chris Scott (Trailblazer Publications, 2008)

Accommodation and Public Transport links

A *Pennine Way: Accommodation and Public Transport Guide* is published by Natural England and available for free download from www.nationaltrail.co.uk/PennineWay/uploads/Text_low.pdf.

DVD

The Pennine Way from the Air (Countryside Agency, now Natural England, nd)

Maps

Ordnance Survey 1:25,000 (2½in to the mile) Explorer Maps
OL1 Dark Peak; OL21 South Pennines; OL10 Yorkshire Dales (South); OL2: Yorkshire Dales (West); OL30 Yorkshire Dales (North & Central); OL31 North Pennines – Teesdale & Weardale; OL43 Hadrian's Wall – Haltwhistle and Hexham; OL42 Kielder Water – Bellingham & Simsonside Hills; OL16 The Cheviot Hills.

Ordnance Survey 1:50,000 (1in to the mile) Landranger Maps
110 Sheffield & Huddersfield; 109 Manchester; 103 Blackburn & Burnley; 98 Wensleydale & Upper Wharfedale; 91 Appleby-in-Westmorland; 92 Barnard Castle & Richmond; 86 Haltwhistle & Brampton; 80 Cheviot Hills & Keilder Water; 74 Kelso & Coldstream.

Harveys 1:40,000 National Trail Maps
Pennine Way South (Edale to Horton-in-Ribblesdale); Pennine Way Central (Horton-in-Ribblesdale to Greenhead); Pennine Way North (Greenhead to Kirk Yelholm).

The waterfall of Hareshaw Linn, near Bellingham.

INDEX